The Subject of Politics
Slavoj Žižek's Political Philosophy

Alternative Formats

This book is also available as a pdf ebook from http://www.Humanities-Ebooks.co.uk and from MyiLibrary.com and as a reflowable ebook from Amazon Kindle and Lulu.com. The pdf is ideal for larger devices such as the Kindle DX, the iPad and the Dell Streak.

The Subject of Politics:
Slavoj Žižek's Political Philosophy

Henrik Jøker Bjerre & Carsten Bagge Laustsen

HEB ☼ Humanities-Ebooks, LLP

Copyright

© Henrik Jøker Bjerre and Carsten Bagge Laustsen, 2010

The Authors have asserted their right to be identified as the author of this Work in accordance with the Copyright, Designs and Patents Act 1988.

This edition published by *Humanities-Ebooks, LLP,*
Tirril Hall, Tirril, Penrith CA10 2JE

ISBN 978-1-84760-169-8 Pdf
ISBN 978-1-84760-170-4 Kindle
ISBN 978-1-84760-179-7 Paperback

Contents

A Note on the Authors	7
Acknowledgements	8
Introduction	9
Chapter 1. Psychoanalysis as a theory of society	**16**
The unconscious	*16*
Back to Lacan	*21*
Discourse analysis or critique of ideology	*24*
You remind me of Emmanuel Ravelli!	*26*
Chapter 2. Žižek's sociology: the ideological fantasm	**32**
We know very well…	*34*
The mirror stage as critique of ideology	*42*
Fetishism as a political form	*46*
The two sides of the social bond	*49*
Chapter 3. Žižek's diagnosis of contemporary society	**54**
The fall of the Father	*55*
Nationalism and ethnic conflicts	*61*
Multiculturalism and racism	*65*
Terrorism and 11 September	*71*
Chapter 4. The revolutionary subject: Žižek's ethical and political horizon	**77**

I think not, therefore I am	*79*
The Proletarian	*86*
*It is the **economy**, stupid!*	*93*
Postmodernism as the new ideological superstructure of capitalism	*96*
St. Paul on the barricade	*99*
Communism, of course!	*102*

Chapter 5. Did somebody say totalitarianism? Žižek's critics. **106**

The rebellion against the father	*107*
Passions of the real	*110*
The useful idiot	*117*

Bibliography **120**

A Note on the Authors

Henrik Jøker Bjerre is Assistant Professor at the Department of Philosophy and History of Ideas, Aarhus University, Denmark. His main research interests are moral philosophy, sociology and psychoanalysis. His publications include *Kantian Deeds* (Continuum, 2010).

Carsten Bagge Laustsen is Associate Professor at the Department of Political Science, Aarhus University, Denmark. His main research interests are terrorism, political theology, political thought and modern social theory. He has previously published *The Culture of Exception. Sociology Facing the Camp* (Routledge, 2005, with Bülent Diken) and *Sociology through the Projector* (Routledge, 2008, with Bülent Diken).

Acknowledgements

The authors wish to thank Stuart Pethick for a much appreciated proof reading of the manuscript and Mark Addis and Richard Gravil at HEB for their patience and good advice.

Introduction

Professor James Miller once remarked on Slavoj Žižek's effect on American academia that, 'He was like Diogenes the Cynic parachuted into the American academy' (Mead 2003: 2). Like Diogenes in ancient Greece, who lived in a barrel and openly displayed his disrespect for any public authority, Žižek sometimes causes a stir because of his provocative statements and unorthodox approaches to the classics of philosophy. He is a philosopher, political thinker, psychoanalyst and sociologist. He is one of the most requested intellectuals in the world, not least because of his poignant and often surprising diagnoses of contemporary society and his very entertaining style. By analysing everything from differences in the construction of toilets in different cultures to mainstream Hollywood productions, and from Hegel's logics to the latest landmarks in neuroscience, Žižek has created a unique ability to keep his audience spellbound.

The enjoyment in reading or listening to Žižek, however, is double-edged. Often you are having an excellent time, while at the same time being told that you are petty bourgeois, narrow minded, racist, evil, or perverted. This somewhat sadomasochistic relation to his audience and readers has turned Žižek into something as rare as an academic superstar. He is a rare showman and constantly surprises by turning a problem upside down ('I agree with you, but my point would be much more radical and *exactly* the opposite'), he draws on endless jokes and examples, and he both writes and talks in an almost manic fashion. 'I discovered, when I was in analysis, that if I stopped talking, the analyst would ask me very unpleasant questions', as he explained at a conference in Sweden in 2002. 'Therefore, I usually continue without pause'.

Slavoj Žižek was born in Ljubljana, Slovenia, on 21 March 1949. He grew up in Tito's Yugoslavia, and received his education from the University of Ljubljana, where he graduated with an MA in philosophy in 1975 with a thesis on post-structuralist French thinkers, after having already published his first book during his education. In spite of his obvious talent, however, he had to settle for an outsider position from the beginning. Because of his charismatic and somewhat rebellious style and his explicit interest in French philosophy, the Yugoslavian authorities were simply uncomfortable with letting him teach, and after serving military duty he had to seek refuge in the Institute of Sociology, via the influence of some friends. In retrospect, however, Žižek has described his difficulties in the years from 1975 to 1979 as a stroke of luck: 'I think that if I were to have got a job at that point, I would now be a poor stupid unknown professor in Ljubljana, probably dabbling in a little bit of Derrida, a little bit of Heidegger, a little bit of Marxism and so on' (Daly/ Žižek 2004: 32–33).

The difficult conditions and the opportunity to continue his work at the sociological institute also forced Žižek to engage more systematically with other areas of thought, such as the sociological and political. Having delivered his Ph.D. thesis in 1981, he moved to Paris to investigate the philosophical and psychoanalytical milieu around Jacques Derrida and Jacques Lacan. Lacan died in 1981, but Žižek nonetheless obtained a very direct training in psychoanalysis through Lacan's son-in-law, Jacques-Alain Miller. Under his supervision, Žižek wrote his second dissertation, this time within psychoanalysis.

After returning to Slovenia, he participated actively in the Slovenian opposition in the years leading up to independence in 1990. A number of philosophers, including Mladen Dolar, Miran Božovič, Renata Salecl, Rado Riha and Jelica Šumič-Riha, participated in both political debates and groundbreaking philosophical initiatives through the Society for Theoretical Psychoanalysis (ANALECTA) in Ljubljana. The circle had a broad intellectual appeal and ties to other fields, like the somewhat enigmatic rock band *Laibach* (the German word for Ljubljana), who exhibited the nationalist overtones of the time in grotesque forms. Žižek ran as a candidate for the presidential elections in 1990 and made an unusual and lively philosophical impact on several of the debates during the campaign. Together with a handful of younger researchers, this group is still today sometimes referred to as 'the Slovenian School', although it is far from forming any consistent unity. A common field of interest can be identified, however, in classic, and especially German, philosophy, Lacanian psychoanalysis, and Marxist critique of ideology. Referring to the 'Slovenian *School*' should nonetheless be taken with a grain of salt, since very few of its 'masters' are doing any actual teaching today, and since significant philosophical and political divergence has occurred among them. In his book on the war in Iraq, Žižek tellingly narrows down his loyalty to 'the two other members of my party *troika*' – Mladen Dolar and Alenka Zupančič (Žižek 2004).

As should already be clear, it is impossible to place Žižek's thinking unambiguously in one category. The fact that he is an analyst of contemporary society, however, is not up for debate. Regardless of the theme he is writing on or talking about, he is always contributing to the understanding of the modern world, and not least its (lacking) politics. Žižek belongs to the group of theoreticians who refuse to accept the dogma of much of the 1980s and 1990s about the death of the 'grand narratives' and the accompanying celebration of the end of history and the final victory of liberal capitalist democracy. For Žižek, the idea of having overcome ideology once and for all is the very epitome of an ideological conviction, and he sees every reason to insist without compromise on a politico-philosophical engagement, especially in our supposedly 'post-political' times. By employing Lacanian psychoanalysis in the diagnosis of contemporary society, he seeks to identify the unacknowledged underside of the liberal political discourse that is reigning in most of the Western world.

Even though one could, with some right, say that 'everything is addressed at once' in Žižek's work, it is possible to extract two main interests: firstly, a strictly philosophical endeavour (which is also politically relevant) to investigate traditional problems like being, subjectivity, and act. Secondly, a more directly political and sociological analysis, a critical thinking with a particular emphasis on articulating the unconscious workings of contemporary political and everyday life, and thereby ideally assisting us in dismantling ingrown ideological convictions that we are not even aware of having.

The philosophical line in Žižek's work could also be characterised as a rereading of classical German philosophy. Immanuel Kant (1724–1804), Georg Wilhelm Friedrich Hegel (1770–1831) and Friedrich Schelling (1775–1854) are constant points of reference, and Žižek's methodological approach to them is explicitly Lacanian. By employing a theoretical framework from Lacan's psychoanalytic work, an opportunity arises to rearticulate some fundamental insights into classic philosophy in contemporary terms. These 'Lacanian interventions' have their role model in Lacan's own analysis of the Cartesian ego, which is also a focal point for Žižek's work (not least in *The Ticklish Subject* from 1999), although Descartes is rarely treated as systematically as the German classics. Like Lacan's, Žižek's readings are intended to articulate unactualised potential in classic philosophical texts, often by bringing out what the authors didn't realise they were saying. Returning to or 'repeating' Descartes, therefore, does not mean putting forward a theory of subjectivity that is based directly on Descartes' own understanding of the *cogito*, but to show the aspects of his thinking that the tradition has not granted sufficient attention, as well as the aspects or consequences which he *himself* did not grant enough attention. The philosophy of subjectivity that emerged from the Cartesian *cogito* and was reinvigorated and radically reinterpreted in Kant's philosophy and in German Idealism, is of particular interest to Žižek, and with it concepts like freedom, act, belief and existence. The analysis of the ground problems in the philosophy of subjectivity is supposed to create the theoretical foundation of the revolutionary subject.

Because he consistently investigates and claims the fundamental importance of the problems of the philosophy of subjectivity, Žižek could be said to be a traditional, and in some sense even a conservative, philosopher. The widespread critique of metaphysics throughout the latter half of the twentieth century in particular has, according to Žižek, thrown out the baby with the dirty water: in the break with the tradition of metaphysics, as it was carried out in, for example, structuralism, psychoanalysis, and the neo-positivist analytical philosophy of language, philosophy has convinced itself to have overcome metaphysical questions in their traditional forms. For Žižek, metaphysics is still produced from such a self-understanding, but it is a bad or unreflective metaphysics. In place of this he sees psychoanalysis as a privileged means to identify more precise metaphysical points in philosophy's allegedly post-metaphysical age. The linguistic and psychoanalytic turns in philosophy since the early part of the twentieth century did not mark the final departure of traditional metaphysical problems; on the contrary, Žižek sees the contemporary situation in philosophy as an opportunity to finally restate the classical problems in their truly radical dimension.

In much the same way one could say that Žižek's opposition to the idea of the end of history and the final victory of the capitalist world-order springs from a (theoretical) conviction that it is precisely after having *traversed* this fantasy that we have the possibility of thinking an entirely new, political project. The post-political situation that has occurred after the fall of the Berlin Wall, and especially the collapse of Eastern European communist regimes, does not therefore mean that we must abandon the radical leftist (or even communist) agenda, on the contrary: the critique of globalised capitalism should enable a universalist, global engagement in favour of a politics that is socialist in a sense that is yet to be seen. The parallel to the more strictly philosophical engagement should thus be clear: 'overcoming' metaphysics/politics makes possible the *renewal* of metaphysics/politics in a sharper version.

Žižek is aggressively opposed to lukewarm ideas of a social democratic third way (à la Blair/Giddens), multiculturalist liberalism, Western Buddhism and so on, i.e. different variants of the resignation of critical thinking: instead of fighting for a global restructuring and political renewal, we are fighting for the recognition of cultural and religious rights, respect for individual autonomy and identity, conservation of parts of the welfare society, environmental lobbyism on behalf of endangered species, and so on. If anyone seeks more than this, or merely insists on the possibility of thinking another possible societal order, a growing tendency has emerged to reject them without any other argument than the postulate of an inherent necessity of disaster in such thinking:

> the moment one shows the slightest inclination to engage in political projects that aim seriously to challenge the existing

order, the answer is immediately: 'Benevolent as it is, this will necessarily end in a new Gulag!' (Žižek 2001a: 3–4)

If Žižek is a 'Diogenes parachuted down', then this also goes for his attitude towards this general academic prohibition of thinking – a prohibition which he often challenges by provoking his audiences at lectures and conferences, but which he also examines in his works by investigating the limits of how far a contemporary political project should actually be ready to go. In questions such as the length to which one should support revolutionary movements, military interventions, the death penalty and so on, Žižek typically turns the problem upside down: if we do not take it on ourselves to rethink the most fundamental political questions, we will be reinforcing a tendency that has grown markedly since 1989 – and indeed since 2001 – where the 'prohibition of thinking' has co-existed with very real assaults, exploitation and war.

In common with the two lines in his thinking, Žižek refuses to accept the end of thinking in any sense, be it metaphysically or politically. The reader and the audience are instead offered a contribution to a kind of literary psychoanalysis: by traversing our age in all its manifold aspects, comparing it directly to the cultural and philosophical inheritance and thereby bringing forward new interpretations of the tradition as well as new perspectives on the situation of the contemporary human being, Žižek wants to point beyond the reality we are living and that which is the most difficult to see past. Psychoanalytically expressed, the purpose is to traverse the fantasy and reach *la passe*: the transformation from the analysed subject to the acting, analysing, creating subject.

In this book, we will introduce Žižek's analysis of contemporary society by means of the following procedure. First, in chapter one, we will elaborate on the relation between psychoanalysis and political thinking. How can it be justified at all to apply a scientific discourse (the scientific status of which is even constantly put in doubt), explicitly developed for the analysis of concrete pathologies in individuals, to the analysis of societal problems? In chapter two, psychoanalysis is put to work in the analysis of the fantasmatic character of ideology: how does Žižek's critique of ideology differ from earlier types of critique, and what role does Lacan play in this? In chapter three, we will look more directly at contemporary society and describe Žižek's diagnosis of four central themes, while in chapter four we will address the potential for breaking with the suppressing and pacifying collective pathologies that we seem to be suffering from. In other words, we shall attempt in short form to frame what could be called Žižek's (psycho-) analytical project: the movement from the interpellated, ideological subject to the creative, revolutionary, acting subject. In a final chapter, we will highlight some of the main criticisms of Žižek that have been articulated during the past 5–10 years in particular.

Chapter 1. Lacanian interventions: Psychoanalysis as a theory of society

In his work, Slavoj Žižek performs a psychoanalytic study of society. What could be meant by this is the theme of this chapter, for couldn't one already simply dismiss his project on this ground? How can it be possible to perform the psychoanalysis of a society, as if there were a common, psychological unconscious – a sort of flipside of the World Spirit – which could be brought forward through some kind of mystical, metaphysical discourse? The first step in the exposition of Žižek's use of psychoanalysis must be to answer this immediate intuition and to show how the unconscious is not, on neither the 'individual' nor social level, an inscrutable, hidden entity that steps forward in analysis. The unconscious is already out there, and it is therefore already socially and linguistically mediated 'in' the individual. The relation between society and subject is already central to psychoanalysis itself, and the application of it in sociology is not therefore supposed to be an invention of a new metaphysical entity, but rather a shift of perspective.

The unconscious

The image of the unconscious as a sort of ghostlike or hidden substance has given psychoanalysis a bad reputation as a form of mysticism in some quarters. Indeed, it may immediately seem like psychoanalysis fails to live up to any standards of science. How can one investigate an object which has no positively given substance? The very idea of an unconscious, some claim, is absurd or at best without any real sense. It makes sense to talk about the not-conscious: that which we have no knowledge of; you could talk of the pre-conscious, i.e. that which we know, but are not currently conscious of (most people know that Madrid is the capital of Spain, even though they rarely think about it). You could also talk about the pre-reflective, such as automatic reactions to situations that are so familiar to us that we no longer have to reflect on them consciously. Indeed, you could even talk about a sort of bodily intelligence, about how phone numbers are 'in the fingers' after some time. But the unconscious is none of this. It is not something conscious that has sunk down into the depth of the soul. And it is not something which surfaces from an original wealth of biological or instinctual appetites – like a sexual need (Hyldgaard 1998: 38f).

The unconscious is unconscious and is not dug out like in an archaeological project. But this does not entail that it is an irrelevant concept or that it is unscientific. The unconscious shows itself – but as 'absent' – as that which punctuates the speech of the analysand as symptoms. The unconscious is the problematic or unfinished in our relation to the world. It shows itself in contexts that we are part of, as signification that we and our behaviour have, but which we are not conscious of. It is meaning that we are creating behind our own backs; that which we are doing without knowing that we are doing it. To illustrate this point, we might make use of a truly Žižekian example.

In one of his many articulations of psychoanalytic points through concrete, historical events, Žižek refers to the former American Secretary of Defence Donald Rumsfeld, who, through a small course of epistemology in 2003, emphasised all the possible dangers that Saddam Hussein represented. Rumsfeld reminded us that 'There are known knowns. These are things we know that we know. There are known unknowns. That is to say, there are things that we know that we don't know. But there are also unknown unknowns. There are things we don't know we don't know' (Žižek 2004: 9). In other words, Rumsfeld pointed to a number of logically possible explanations of the ways in which Iraq posed a threat, including that which we 'don't know that we don't know'. Not only did we know that Saddam had WMDs before (known knowns), and that we did not know everything about their present whereabouts (known unknowns), but we might very well also imagine that there were even things that we didn't suspect, i.e. that he was hiding secretly obtained weapons in facilities entirely unknown to us (unknown unknowns).

Žižek points out that Rumsfeld forgot the fourth possible combination of the known and the unknown: the unknown knowns, namely that which we don't know that we know, 'which is precisely the Freudian unconscious, the "knowledge which does not know itself", as Lacan used to say' (ibid.: 9–10). Rumsfeld and co. knew more than they knew: in their actions a type of knowledge was present, which did not know itself, about the motives for invading Iraq and the consequences it would have. The unacknowledged knowledge, e.g. the idea of the superiority of Western civilisation and its right to intervene where it finds it timely, in a way returned in its perverted form with the disclosure, around a year after the invasion, of the torture and humiliation that had taken place in American controlled prisons in Iraq.

The unconscious is thus a type of knowledge, but is rather unlike what we ordinarily understand by knowledge. It would not be advisable to rely on the unconscious in a game of Jeopardy. It is what we do not know that we know, i.e. a way that we act or place ourselves in the world without being aware of the implications. Therefore, the horizon of meaning that we move in is always broader than we think. The unconscious is structured like a language, as Lacan says, but it is not yet articulated *to* the analysand *as* an understandable message. It is the relations we stand in without being aware of it; it is the fact that we do not oversee our own world and its connections or how our own speech relates to the big picture. A symptom is therefore an immediately incomprehensible message that must be interpreted in order to make sense. It must be placed in a meaningful context that is not yet clear to the analysand, but which she nonetheless – with assistance from the analyst – has the resources to clear up.

The analytical sequence has, as its purpose, to uncover how the analysand 'lives her world' (Žižek 1997: 29). One could say that it is the unacknowledged relations to others that are the theme of analysis. The hypothesis of the unconscious is therefore precisely that which connects the poles of the individual and society. It is because the individual is never complete or master in its own house that it must identify with socially mediated roles and values. The unconscious refers to a constitutive lack of being, which on the one hand forces the individual to ever new acts of identification, while these, on the other hand, will always misfire. The psychoanalyst listens to the ways in which the analysand cultivates this constitutive lack.

The exchange between the psychic and the social can, however, also be analysed from the other side. Just as the subject is driven towards the social, so the social is driven towards its subjects. Society itself is constituted with a lack. 'There is', as Margaret Thatcher put it, 'no such thing as society'. Any regime needs to ensure legitimacy and backing, and this cannot be achieved exclusively through the display of physical power, which would be a self-defeating strategy in the long run, but must also be supported, arguably primarily, by ideology. The function of ideology is to make it possible for the individual to mirror itself in society – like one of the faithful sons of the nation, for example. But why does ideology work? The critique of ideology has turned to psychoanalysis, because here it has found a theory of the constitution of the 'psychic' and an answer to the question of why people identify with ideologies that seem to work against their own interests. Lacan's version of Mrs. Thatcher's refusal of the existence of society could be said to be his famous description of the 'big Other': it does not exist, but it functions nonetheless. There is not, or at least there certainly doesn't *have* to be, any unequivocal conspiracy (a mastermind) behind the way ideologies work on their subjects, but they nonetheless function and subjects largely orient themselves via an imagined coherence behind the actual events in society, or to put it another way: we behave as if there were a society. There *is* no society, but it functions nonetheless.

It is thus possible to focus on the pressure that society exerts on the individual or on the ways in which the individual deals with or handles this pressure. The latter is the task of the psychoanalytic clinic, while the former is the task that psychoanalytically founded social theory has taken on itself. Where clinical psychoanalysis is intrigued by the statements of the individual patient, psychoanalytically founded social theory deals with and is intrigued by social phenomena. In other words, you must always place brackets somewhere:

in clinical psychoanalysis, the brackets are placed around the 'societal', and in psychoanalytically founded social theory, brackets are placed around the 'individual'.

We may thus already confront one of the criticisms that has been levelled against the attempts at employing psychoanalysis within the field of social science. It is said that psychoanalysis is irrelevant because it is interested in individual beings and the motivations that the individual has for his or her actions, and that this might be of interest to psychiatrists, psychologists, and psychoanalysts, while social science is interested in society. Similarly, psychoanalysis has been charged with biologism, pan-sexualism, naturalism and determinism, based on the perception that psychoanalysis conceives the individual as shaped by pre-social forces (ibid. 8). Accordingly, Freud was supposedly blind to the intersubjective and linguistic context within which the individual unfolds itself. This criticism, however, is running in open doors. The forces that are permeating the individual are precisely socially mediated.

An isolated individual subject, for instance, cannot fantasise about a specific, desired object. The question is, as Žižek puts it in *The Plague of Fantasies*, how the subject knows at all that it desires this specific object. How has it learned what an object is, and that precisely this object is desirable? According to Žižek, one cannot say that an 'independent' subject recognises an object in the world as a possible satisfaction of a corresponding pre-linguistic desire, on the contrary: we *learn* to see certain things as desirable or interesting, because we are already part of a socially articulated game of desire. The example Žižek uses to illustrate this is a story Freud himself tells about his daughter Anna, who, at an age where she hardly had any language, was fantasising about strawberry cake one night in her sleep (Freud 1999: 135). Žižek explains this fantasising as an illustration of the fundamentally intersubjective character of desire: the daughter had discovered that her parents enjoyed watching her eating strawberry cake. This feeling of doing something that fulfilled the strong wish in the parents to see their child in a certain way, created a very strong emotional attachment to strawberry cake in the little Anna. She learned to desire strawberry cake because she thereby achieved the status of being the object of the desire of the other(s) – her parents. She became the happy, enjoying little girl whom they loved (to watch) (Žižek 1997: 9). This story illustrates that desire, in Lacan's words, is always the desire of the other. What I desire is first and foremost to be desired by the other, i.e. to become or do something which the other finds love-able. Even the most 'immediate' private wish is therefore always already mediated by a kind of unconscious awareness of our relations to the other. In a most literal sense there is no psychic private language.

Back to Lacan

Jacques Lacan's reinterpretation of or 'return' to Freud has given psychoanalysis a new fruitfulness to a range of theoretical fields, and Slavoj Žižek has contributed with one of the most influential translations of this potential in the field of social theory. Lacan is primarily known as the one who brought the linguistic turn to psychoanalysis, and he is simultaneously one of the central figures in French post-structuralism. The dominant reading of Freud in Lacan's time was one of ego-psychology, and in order to salvage psychoanalysis from the individualistic misconceptions of this tradition, Lacan claimed that the road back to Freud had to go through the structural linguistics of Ferdinand de Saussure. Hence Lacan's description of the unconscious as 'structured like a language'. Only in this way could the radicality of Freud be preserved. Lacan wanted to add a more strict, structuralist awareness of language to Freud's groundbreaking clinical observations. With Lacan the intersubjective foundation of psychoanalysis is unfolded, thereby rendering it relevant for sociology; with Žižek, it becomes political.

Social science has always imported from neighbouring disciplines. In this sense, there is nothing controversial about Žižek's mixture of philosophy, psychoanalysis and sociology. Exactly by 'bracketing' the particular, unique individual and its handling of societal pressure, and focusing on the games of meaning, power and desire that are displayed in the public and political space, Lacanianism can contribute to new ways of articulating and questioning the political. Central

22 The Subject of Politics

to this work is, for Žižek, the concept of the subject, and it is in the exploration of a concept of the subject relevant to social thinking that he combines (classical, mainly German) philosophy with psychoanalysis. By investigating the universalist implications of the classical concept of the subject and combining it with the perspectives of the social field in psychoanalysis, Žižek seeks to establish a more refined understanding of how subjectivity is at stake in our age, as well as seeking, in a very broad sense of the word, a kind of therapy to overcome some of the pathological elements in it.

In a first take, one could simply say that in psychoanalysis Žižek seeks new ways of framing the questions that may contribute to a more adequate understanding of society. By employing a strategy of questioning similar to the one which is unfolded in the analytical situation, attention can be directed towards parts of our societal reality that are not commonly addressed, or it can be directed towards that which makes us act or refrain from acting in certain ways, and what makes us accept ideological constructions and see ourselves the way we do. Psychoanalysis as a strategy for questioning can, as Danish scholar Lilian Munk Rösing has put it, help us to consider a fundamental question: 'what if things are really working in exactly the opposite way of how we commonly take them to work?'

> What if the client, who states that she loves men, thereby also says the opposite, namely that she hates them? What if the slogan of Coca Cola that 'this is it' also means the opposite – that it is precisely *not* it: Coca Cola is never the fully satisfying object. And what if this is precisely the reason why we have to keep on buying it? What if Tony Blair's 'third way' simultaneously indicates the opposite: that there is really only one way – the one of liberalism? What if the Western pluralistic ideology of freedom is simultaneously the opposite: a homogenising culture of commodification? (Rösing 2005: 103, our translation)

It is noticeable that Žižek, in both his writing and talks, again and again makes use of exactly this form of questioning: 'what if...?' Often, one can simply read these what-ifs as straightforward claims. When

Žižek writes 'what if', he usually means 'in reality, the fact of the matter is this…'. As interventions in polite, coherent, academic discourse, Žižek's questions are almost always intrusive inversions. His method in this sense is a type of forced application of psychoanalysis to social scientific themes. With Gilles Deleuze, one could talk of a kind of activism of concepts in this approach to social theory. By not merely describing an available, understandable reality, but actively investigating it, challenging it and inverting it, the very attempt at mapping and understanding becomes a theoretical contribution itself. The writing becomes a labyrinth that forces the reader to find his or her own way. The Lacanian interventions become reinterpretations intended to make the reader reconsider and think, i.e. to see his or her own age in a new light and thereby also acquire a new approach to his or her own position in the societal order: what if…?

Lacan's concepts are mostly formal abstractions, which means that they have to be reformulated in every context. When psychoanalysis is employed in its social theoretical variant this entails that a particular type of diagnostic sensitivity must be developed. This partly means that Žižek's critics are in a certain sense *always* right: there is no one unequivocal, corresponding method for the application of Lacan's conceptual structures to contemporary philosophical and political themes. There *is* no big Other that acts in such-and-such a specific way, and there is no proto-subject that identifies unequivocally in terms of this acting. Nonetheless, psychoanalysis can be put to work to throw light on issues which are difficult to handle in statistical, rationalist and other analytical strategies. Psychoanalysis has developed a series of formal structures to identify forms of suffering and being such as hysteria, neurosis, perversion, fetishism, etc. This in turn leads to more specific analyses of conditions like anxiety, narcissism, and stress, as well as phenomena like objectification, alienation, nationalism, racism, commodity fetishism, etc. For Žižek, such analyses make possible a more nuanced understanding of the pressure that a specific political system, *in casu* capitalism, exerts on its subjects.

Discourse analysis or critique of ideology

Lacan's thinking, together with that of Derrida, Deleuze, Foucault and other French philosophers from the 1960s onwards (all of which has been central to Žižek's thinking from the beginning), has formed the basis of what is usually referred to as post-structuralism. In the social sciences, this broad theoretical field is often propagated under the banners of discourse analysis and social constructivism. One often refers to a 'linguistic turn', on the background of which the analytical focus is redirected towards investigations of textual and verbal expressions. In its most radical forms, discourse analysis has developed into a radical empiricism. The idea of something 'behind' concrete texts and statements is rejected. What *is* is what is articulated: the concrete expressions.

Lacan's thinking, as well as Žižek's, works against what one could call a discourse analytical reductionism. It is true that the subject is necessarily permeated, and to some extent alienated, by language, but the alienation in symbolic and imaginary identities does not exhaust it. The 'more' or the remainder, which insists after the socialisation of the subject, is the ground of psychoanalysis. It is described as the subject of the unconscious. Psychoanalysis is about all that which is *not* articulated in discourses, consciousness, cultures, self-perceptions, etc., but which is nonetheless there, if in no other sense than as the necessary, material background or the place for these articulations.

But how does one conceptualise the foundation of a critical practice (which seeks an additional 'more' to that which is to be found in explicit evidence of cultural etc. norms) in such a way that it does not become a particularism? Clinical practice has a fundamentally critical aim: it seeks to make people better. And this ambition, obviously, cannot be met without a thorough reflection on the conditions for a better life. One should not 'cede upon one's desire' – one is encouraged to 'traverse the fantasm', etc. These fundamental moral intuitions are transported into the social scientific version of psychoanalysis, although there are of course differences between focusing on the sufferings of an individual patient and on the societal conditions that provoke them. One cannot infer directly from the societal to the 'individual'.

As a program statement for a Lacanian critique of ideology, one could say that it investigates how different identifications are possible and encouraged within the social field, while simultaneously examining the background of the instability and possibly radical change that might occur exactly because of tension within the process of identification itself. Fundamentally, it is of course worth noticing that we are talking about ideologies rather than discourses. The perspective of the critique of ideology is different from the one of discourse analysis in that it does not see social reality as a complex game of competing discourses, but rather as founded upon one overarching frame of reference. Of course, alternative and competing perspectives are present in many important senses, but the emphasis is on one, overall, structuring perspective. The dominant ideology manifests the ability of the ruling class to make their values count in order to support and cement their social position. The other important difference is that the critique of ideology differentiates between the dimension of contents and the dimension of enunciation. Although ideology produces subject positions, this does not mean that there is no one who benefits from its yields. This approach to the analysis of ideology is not to be found within the frame of discourse analysis. Here, the subject is not something that is 'behind' a statement, but exclusively something that is produced in the statement. In fact it is both, as we shall see later.

In spite of the relativisation that inevitably comes with the linguistic turn, Žižek insists that it is still possible to be critical in a more fundamental sense than discourse analysis: there is such a thing as oppression, we can operate with a truth which puts the content of ideologies into perspective, and so on. One could perhaps explain this more precisely by differentiating between two different concepts of truth. The truth that is generated in knowledge as we commonly understand it is a truth that can be collected in heaps of data, as in propositions with a well defined semantic content where the content of knowledge corresponds to a reality that is independent of the knower. Truth in the sense that Žižek is after, on the other hand, is that which allows another reality or another dimension of reality to step forward.

Discourse analysis often establishes a sort of prohibition against asking ontological questions – it tends to reduce ontology to epistemology, or more generally, it relativises the fundamental philosophical and political questions to the historical and cultural contexts within which they emerged. Typically, we find variants of the convictions that there is no such thing as society, but only multiple discourses, there is no such thing as Woman, but only white, middle class women, black single mothers, lesbians, etc., and there are no classes, but only groups ordered by consumption or lifestyles (Žižek 1999: 133). This approach precisely obscures the type of truth that Žižek wants to bring forward in his analyses:

> [W]hen a typical Cultural Theorist deals with a philosophical or psychoanalytic edifice, the analysis focuses exclusively on unearthing its hidden patriarchal, Eurocentrist, identitarian, etc., 'bias', without even asking the naive but none the less necessary question: OK, but what *is* the structure of the universe? How does the human psyche 'really' work? Such questions are not even taken seriously in Cultural Studies, since they simply tend to reduce them to historicist reflection upon conditions in which certain notions emerged as a result of historically specific power relations. (Žižek 2001a: 218)

Psychoanalysis offers a critical perspective that does not appear in discourse analysis. It can make explicit a conditioning level that goes deeper than historical, cultural and linguistic conditions. Compared to the descriptions of intersubjective systems found in discourse analysis, psychoanalysis therefore appears as a transcendental philosophical investigation of the subject.

You remind me of Emmanuel Ravelli!

The concept of the subject is one of the most disputed and ambiguous concepts in the tradition of the humanities. It finds its classical stipulation in the juxtaposition of a subject and an object, with the subject as the active part, and the object as something which is acted upon. You can be reduced to being the object of someone's manipulation – a plastic material shaped in the hands of others. You can be an object of strategies, planning, and political action in the broadest sense. The object, of course, is not necessarily another person; it might as well be, and indeed more precisely is, nature in the widest sense. Nature is objectified, it is subjected to scientific scrutiny, and thereby becomes possible to mould. A subject thus capable of moulding its surroundings – whether it be other people, culture or nature in a broader sense – is often referred to as 'an individual', 'a self', 'an I', or more abstractly, 'a human being'. By an individual we understand, negatively, something unique, not moulded or produced, something in-dividual, i.e. indivisible, and if understood positively, something with a consciousness of its own, an ability for reflection, and thereby an ability to act freely and autonomously. In contrast to animals, we have the ability to transcend our most immediate instincts.

What the concept of the individual refers to is something that is identical to itself or less cryptically and more precisely: 'The concept of the individual points to the idea that there are layers and qualities that can be peeled off, while something remains which is indivisible, and this indivisible core must be something that remains the same, i.e. something identical to itself' (Mortensen 2003, our translation). This entirely individual quality refers to that which ties a life history together, i.e. that which remains the same in all contexts and at all times. The 'I' is a kind of hook, on to which all masks, roles, and experiences can be attached. The 'I' is that which remains, once every positive identity has been deducted. The intuition that one is always more than the concrete roles, one performs, and the norms, one is following, is the fundamental intuition to which the concepts of the 'I', the 'individual' and the 'self' refer. This entity is the subject that we know from the liberal tradition and from humanism: an accountable subject that can be held responsible, feel guilt, reflect, and not the least act.

But there is also another subject, or rather another meaning of being a subject, and this time one that relates to the exact opposite, namely to being subjected to the power of others (*sub-jectum*), and, more generally, subjected to social moulding (hence, for instance, the regular discussions of subject positions in structural Marxism). 'Sub-

' here refers to an epi-phenomenon: one is a subjectivised, receiving being. We have here, in other words, the subject which is referred to in sociology: the socialised individual that only exists because of the 'societal'. Structures shape the individual; indeed, the very idea of an individual is something that is socially produced. Sociology, and more narrowly structuralism, thus rejects the understanding of the self as given in an absolute self-presence. This thought is often formulated as an attack on Descartes' *cogito*, which is claimed to have been one of the most radical formulations of a metaphysics of the self, i.e. the idea of a self-transparent I equal to itself (*'cogito ergo sum'*) as the stable basis of a controlling scientific practice that keeps being under control by means of thinking. (Lacan's reading of Descartes' cogito is radically different, and we will encounter this reading in chapter 4).

Structuralism rejects the Cartesian conception of an unproblematic separation of two independently identifiable substances (*res cogitans* and *res extensa*), i.e. the thinking and the extended substance, which can be directly referred to through their immediately representative signs (indexicals). Meaning, according to structuralism, is given from the relations between signs, and not from reference that these signs are supposedly making to the world or to the self. Since language is given as a structural nexus between signs, this also means that the sign never rests in itself, but only carries meaning via its relations to other signs. Thinking does not presuppose a *cogito*, but a system of relations between signs that precedes the thinking agent.

It is obvious that the Cartesian as well as the purely structuralist understanding of what it means to be a subject is of a reductive nature: the subject is either self-present and independent from the world or given entirely in virtue of its linguistic and intersubjective situation. The question here, however, is how different the two conceptions really are. In both cases, being a subject is thought as a coherent and fully given being. The difference between them is that this being has its source in the I or the self according to the liberal and humanist tradition, while in the structuralist tradition it is thought of as derived. The consequence of the criticism that structuralism levels at the Cartesian paradigm is, in other words, not carried through radically enough. Classical structuralism does not identify an absence where liberalism and humanism saw absolute self-presence. It merely replaces a self-presence with a culturally and historically produced presence.

Post-structuralism and especially psychoanalysis here become interesting as a tradition that has taken up the consequence of the critique from structuralism (this is precisely what the 'post' in post-structuralism indicates). Psychoanalysis, for Žižek, exactly represents a way to overcome the dichotomy between the ontologies of presence in the liberalist and the structuralist humanist traditions. Thinking the subject as the subject of the unconscious enables psychoanalysis to maintain the valuable aspects of the Cartesian *cogito* and the conception of the subject in German Idealism, while at the same acknowledging the radical structuralist critique of them. Where the two humanist traditions understand the subject in terms of a personal or social identity, Lacanian psychoanalysis is characterised by understanding the individual or the self as permeated by forces and registers which it does not master itself, and, no less importantly, by forces that are often in a contradictory relation to each other: the self-preservation instinct vs. the death drive, the reality principle vs. the pleasure principle, the superego vs. the id, and so on. One could say that the subject in psychoanalysis is precisely the conflict between the two aspects of subjectivity that the liberal and the structuralist tradition are accentuating. The subject is the unfinished conflict between self-presence and the symbolic identity ensured or given by others.

Žižek enjoys employing jokes from the old Marx Brothers movies and radio plays to illustrate even very abstract theoretical points such as this. One of these jokes nicely illustrates the 'third subject', i.e. subjectivity, as that which is not a pre-symbolic identity, nor the symbolically interpellated subject that is entirely exhausted in its name. Two people meet, and one exclaims: 'Hey! You remind me of Emmanuel Ravelli!' 'But I *am* Emmanuel Ravelli', the other replies, a little bit confused. 'Then no wonder that you look like him!' The conviction of Emmanuel Ravelli that he really is Emmanuel Ravelli illustrates the presumed self-presence of the subject. 'You remind of Emmanuel Ravelli', on the other hand, illustrates the intersubjective identity of the subject, as given by others or by 'the big Other' – *it* will decide whether or not Ravelli is really Ravelli. It is not surprising, of course, that the two look like each other, but the apparently meaningless punch line in the Marx Brothers' joke nonetheless illustrates a minimal distance between them. This distance is the third subject of psychoanalysis.

Although psychoanalysis thus presents itself as the science of this third subject – the subject of the unconscious – this does not entail a negligence of the two other forms of subjectivity. Lacan formulates the three subjects in a topographic field: as three dimensions that are all important in understanding the subject's being in the world. Instead of the 'I', he speaks of the imaginary, which shortly said refers to the ability of saying 'I' – the image of a centre, without which the subject would not be able to create a narrative about its being in the world, and which is thereby also the precondition for connecting experiences together and reflecting on them. Instead of the conception of the subject in social science, and more specifically in structuralism, Lacan speaks of the symbolic: the moulds that are necessary for an identity to be shaped at all. And finally, he speaks of the real, as, on the one hand, the remainder that stays once the subject has identified itself, and, on the other hand as the very impetus behind our engagement in acts of identification. Without a constitutive lack, there is no urge for identification. 'The Real', thus, does not refer to the really existing, but much more to the opposite: to that which always escapes.

Insofar as the subject of the unconscious is the starting point for psychoanalysis and Žižek's thinking, it is a subject that is articulated in the minimal distance of the individual towards itself, or in the lack of completeness that shines through the symbolic and imaginary identities. The very cause of wonder, critique and questioning of societal processes of identification is the driving force in Žižek's psychoanalytically mediated philosophical investigations. When his works do not clearly mark the transition from the individual to the societal level, this is because the transition isn't as clear cut as one might think. The subject is oriented towards society and vice versa. It is this intersection between the individual and the societal that intrigues

Žižek. The closing remarks of this chapter must therefore, by way of a conclusion, emphasise that in order to understand his particular form of social scientific thinking, one must not only try to relocate the methodological procedures of the psychoanalytic clinic in the analysis of societal issues, but also seek to grasp an understanding of subjectivity in general, which encompasses the individual as well as the universal or societal, i.e. which can be applied to individual pathologies as well as to societal conflicts and power structures. It is no coincidence that the critique of ideology plays such a decisive role in the work of Slavoj Žižek.

Chapter 2. The ideological fantasm: Žižek's sociology

Žižek's mixture of philosophy and psychoanalysis has very special advantages for the analysis and critique of political ideology. Even though Žižek is a philosopher, his ambition is not to develop a positive philosophical theory of, for example, justice in any traditional sense, but rather to expand the field of sociological considerations with a Lacanian psychoanalytic perspective in order to make it possible to bring forward the unacknowledged levers that are accompanying political rhetoric and action. It is from this analysis that the 'positive' is supposed to emerge, i.e. in the shape of a production of new opportunities for the understanding of what is socially possible. Žižek is in this sense a Hegelian: it is the determinate negation that creates the possibility of a new form of society or consciousness. It is by analysing the present that one may find the opening that points ahead.

If instead one rushes on with good ideas for political change and aims deducted from a set of initial premises, one will not be able to transcend the fundamental mechanisms that one is embedded in. Within political theory, just as in other fields, one might therefore distinguish between analytical philosophers (such as John Rawls), who wish to develop an a priori theory of justice, legal principles, politics of distribution, etc., and *psycho*analytical philosophers, who take their point of departure in concrete, societal problems and examples on the background of highly elaborated theoretical approaches to the human being from classical philosophy and psychoanalysis in particular. Žižek, so to speak, jumps over the middle link and moves directly from the highest metaphysical theory to the most common, everyday problems, and vice versa.

A nice example of such abrupt leaps from the most profane to the general and theoretical is his consideration of how the different designs of toilets in Germany, France, and England reflect the national character of these three countries: German conservatism and thoroughness (shit is lying open for inspection on a small plateau before being flushed), French revolutionary haste (just flush it!), and English moderate liberalism (a plateau with a bit of water, but no excessive display – just get rid of it in an orderly way). This 'analysis' does bear the characteristics of a slightly racist joke and is based on Erica Jong's provocative statement that 'German toilets are really the key to the horrors of the Third Reich. People who can build toilets like this are capable of anything'. But it does nonetheless rather elegantly illustrate Žižek's point in relation to ideology critique's focus on what we are actually doing, rather on what we are claiming to be doing or should be doing. 'So it is easy for an academic to claim at a round table that we live in a post-ideological universe – the moment he visits the restroom after the heated discussion, he is again knee-deep in ideology' (Žižek 1997: 5).

When, in the Marxist and critical traditions, one often draws on psychoanalytical insight, this is partly because it makes it possible to not only analyse the distribution of assets, for example – who gets what and when – but also the ways in which policies are legitimated. The difference to 'bourgeois' or liberal theories is that legitimisation is regarded as a political process. Legitimation of political decisions is often understood in the light of the concept of ideology. The task of psychoanalysis in this context has been to explain how ideology can be effective in relation to the subject's economy of drives, desires, passions and enjoyment.

The social structure of desire means that the subject is always on the lookout for that which may fulfil his or her desire. The desire is always the desire of the other, i.e. because desire is socially structured, the subject must seek to fulfil its desire by becoming that which the other desires. Without end, the question arises: what does the other want from me? What must I do in order to fulfil my need to be recognised/loved/desired by the other? And any answer is preliminary. The longing for the little object (the *objet a* in Lacanian terms) that embodies that which was missing in order to make possible a harmonic, whole subjective identity (worthy of recognition), is the very

34 The Subject of Politics

driving force in the libidinal economy.

As we shall see later on, the entrance into the symbolic order (language, family, society) is experienced at one and the same time as the establishment of an individual identity, *and* as the loss of the real or original identity. Something is foreign to the subject, a lack of being is always rankling, and it is this lack which constantly forces the subject to new attempts at identifying itself. The subject is always haunted by a lack or a minimal difference between its self-perception and its symbolic mandate. This difference creates the imagination of a 'real' self – which is really a subject without content or a 'barred subject', as Lacan puts it, which only emerges with the symbolic mandate and the accompanying sense that this cannot be all there is to say. For Žižek, the attraction of ideologies can be explained by their offering the subject a scenario for a completion of desire, i.e. they make it possible for subjects to cover their lack of being. The legitimisation of the suppression and exploitation of a hegemonic power is thus possible, because ideology creates particular effects in the libidinal economy of the subjects. One of the most important projects in Žižek's work is to renew the critique of ideology. This chapter will give an account of Žižek's understanding of the concept of an ideological fantasm and put it into perspective in comparison to other classical understandings of what ideology is and how critique of ideology is conducted.

We know very well ...

Traditionally, ideologies have been identified as systems of ideas which communicate incorrect representations of reality: an imagined idea or a system of beliefs that did not match the actual states of affairs. The task of the critique of ideology was accordingly seen as correcting these false representations through enlightenment. No matter how intensely this representationalist approach has been criticised, it has proven to be remarkably tenacious. When ideologies are often taken, in public discourse, to be something outdated, rigid and naïve, it should be seen in this context: as a continuation of the conviction that ideologies are misrepresentations of a reality, which 'should' simply be described with commonsense and an unbiased approach. However, it has been clear for a long time that 'false' ideas (false in their objective content) are not necessarily ideological, just as 'true' ideas might very well be ideological in a fundamental sense (Žižek 1993a: 230–231).

Ideologies were later taken to be false because of the position from which they were enounced. Ideologies were 'false', if they were functional in the creation and legitimisation of relations of social dominance and exploitation. The function of ideologies was to hide or cover these relations. The critique of ideology in this perspective was typically a Marxist one that attempted to analyse and uncover the relations of dominance that were hidden by hegemonic systems of ideas, and then to make people conscious of them. The thesis was that the work of ideology had to be kept hidden in order to function and that it thus couldn't be maintained, once openly displayed (Žižek 1994a: 8).

The struggle was therefore not fought against ideas that were scientifically untrue, but against a false consciousness of the social world. Enlightenment now aimed at enlightening workers about social reality, i.e. capitalist exploitation, in order to unite them in a common struggle. The criticisms of this perspective are many: its focus on consciousness misses the point that ideologies are manifested in social practices; the representationalist approach presupposes a non-ideological layer of reality behind the ideological; it is difficult to trace emancipatory potential when false consciousness prevails; and finally it is precisely when one claims to be talking objectively, neutrally and attempting to resist critique, that one is performing an ideological operation. The most important critique, however, is that the ethical foundation of the different conceptions of ideology as false consciousness consist in an imagination of an irreversible emancipation through enlightenment and the installation of an ideal of ever more enlightened and rational subjects that will ultimately be able to free themselves from ideology as such. The success of the critique of ideology was thus supposed to render it superfluous.

The problem is, among other things, that this form of enlightenment has merely paved the way for an even more subtle form of ideology that is ironic in its relation to its own truth value. The problem does not now seem to be false consciousness, but enlightened false consciousness. We know very well that we are commodity fetishists, that God is dead, that nations are political constructions and so on, but we nonetheless insist on these ideas in our everyday practice as if they were final and true. Why this cynicism? To begin to answer this question, one must start by acknowledging that more than the merely discursive is at stake when we identify with ideological configurations. The need to address this 'more' than the purely discursive is what makes psychoanalytically inspired critique of ideology particularly strong. In Freudo-Marxism, the 'more' was primarily drives, while in a Lacanian perspective it is desire and enjoyment.

The three approaches to the critique of ideology just sketched represent three different understandings of the relation between reality and the reflection of it. One could categorise them through the triad of realism, modernism, and postmodernism (Žižek 1996: 233, n. 16). In realism, reality has a structure and nature of its own independently from reflection and the experience of it. This conviction can be found in classical pre-Marxist conceptualisations of ideology, which saw it as their task to fight unscientific ideas. Modernism (e.g. Lukács) believes in the liberating power of reflection and its ability to change its object (consciousness). This is the foundation of the Marxist paradigm, according to which enlightenment will make possible a change in consciousness and thereby work for the demolition of the existing structures of dominance. Postmodernism, in Žižek's version, goes a step further and claims that ideologies are maintained precisely through a reflective distance, and that it is through our non-identification with the configurations of ideology that we make them possible.

Žižek's critique of ideology is about the disclosure of the cynical, reflective distance to ideology as a hidden or unspoken approval of it. By ironically dismantling our relation to ideology (state, party, market), we let it function in practice, i.e. we 'distance ourselves' from the effects of a real antagonism, which we can thereby simultaneously support in virtue of the position we hold in society. The effect is, Žižek claims, that ideology ends up functioning in exactly the opposite way that traditional critique imagined: 'Ideology is not a dreamlike illusion that we build to escape insupportable reality; in its basic dimension it is a fantasy-construction which serves as a support for our 'reality' itself' (Žižek 1989: 45). The critique of ideology, in other words, makes it apparent that given ideological constructions rest on a repression of the antagonistic character of society. The task is therefore not to show that ideologies misrepresent reality, which is the modernist gesture, but to show how the very idea of a reality behind the ideological mask is an illusion. Ideologies are not representations, but the very anchor of social reality. The imagination of moving beyond ideologies by 'being conscious of them' therefore actually shows our submission to them.

> [T]here is more truth in a mask than in what is hidden beneath it: a mask is never simply 'just a mask' since it determines the actual place we occupy in the intersubjective symbolic network; what is effectively false and null is our 'inner distance' from the mask we wear (the 'social role' we play), our 'true self' hidden beneath it. The performative dimension at work here consists of the symbolic efficiency of the 'mask': wearing a mask actually *makes us* what we feign to be. (Žižek 1992a: 34)

It is the very idea of a difference between the mask and the true self behind it which is an illusion. By insisting that our inner kernel is something else than the mask we are carrying in everyday life, we might convince ourselves that we hold ideology at arms length, but therein resides the illusion. We know very well that we are participating in objective mechanisms that structure the design of our political world, but we are not *really* involved in it, because it is not our personal, conscious goal to support the precise concrete consequences that follow from how society is designed. We here encounter Žižek's rejection of what he often refers to as Western Buddhism: we work hard and without reflecting too much on what we are doing as busy little bees in an exploiting, suppressing, and environmentally degrading system, but it is not 'really' us who partake in it – only our public mask. In the evening, when we come home and put down the mask, we can spend some quality time with our children and meditate on our pure eternal soul, Nirvana, or other types of New Age escapism. Žižek, however, maintains that there is a place from which ideologies can be criticised. Such a place is necessary, but he insists that one cannot or should not try to give it a positive content. In his own words:

> [A]lthough no clear line of demarcation separates ideology from reality, although ideology is already at work in everything we experience as 'reality', we must none the less maintain the tension that keeps the *critique* of ideology alive. Perhaps, following Kant, we could designate this impasse the 'antinomy of critic-ideological reason': ideology is not all; it is possible to assume a place that enables us to maintain a distance from it, *but this place from which one can denounce ideology must remain empty, it cannot be occupied by any positively determined reality* – the moment we yield to this temptation, we are back in ideology. (Žižek 1994a: 17)

When Žižek refers to Kant here, he is hinting at and repeating the movement that Kant makes in his first two critiques from 1781 and 1788 respectively, (*Critique of Pure Reason* and *Critique of Practical Reason*). Kant explicitly considers it to be the distinguished result of his theoretical philosophy not to have 'filled out the empty place' that was left from the lacking completion of the metaphysical ambition of reaching a coherent and whole description of the origin, boundaries and purpose of the world. This 'empty place' is in turn occupied by the moral law (the categorical imperative), which always confronts us with a moral responsibility, but never allows for a 'final' description of wherein this responsibility consists, or in other words, it never provides us with a manual for right moral behaviour. One could say that the 'lacking' stability of the ontological order, which theoretical philosophy ended up identifying, made way for an imperative to subjects with the ability to reason that we ourselves establish a meaningful universal order: act as if you could want the maxim of your action to be universal law – but do not pretend to have thereby solved the *theoretical* problem of the unity and meaning of the world. In this sense Kant, seen with Žižek's eyes, was not only a critical philosopher, but a critic of *ideology* as well.

More concretely, the task of philosophy for both Kant and Žižek is not to legitimise power, but to pose questions to it. On the front page of the book *Tarrying with the Negative* (Žižek 1993a), Žižek even gives this point a material expression by using a photo of the Romanian flag after the 1989 military coup against former dictator Nicolae Ceauşescu. In the photo, the red star in the Romanian flag has been cut out to demonstrate the break with the old system, but it thereby simultaneously perfectly illustrates the role of the critique of ideology: it is this empty place that critique must keep open.

But back to the question: what is the driving force behind the identification with the configuration of some particular ideology? The answer, according to Žižek, is that ideologies are fantasies about the fulfilment of our desire, and that they are promising or hinting at an exceptional, or sublime, state of being. Or maybe more precisely: with its tacit promises, the fantasm is that which teaches us how to desire. For Lacan, desire is what distinguishes us as humans – not in the sense of our ability to desire particular objects, but in the sense that our desire is structured by and directed towards the desire of another human being. We desire that others desire us, as it was displayed in the story about the appetite for strawberry cakes in little Anna Freud.

One could make this point more explicit by differentiating between desire and need. Need is defined as that which you are aware that you lack, while the object of desire is not positively given. The human being not only exists as a creature with (simple) needs to fulfil. It also seeks and demands recognition, which means that it desires the desire of the other. Where needs are concrete and can be met, desire is metonymical and never allows to be fulfilled through the acquisition of this or that particular object. Any object is an inadequate stand-in for the complete satisfaction of the desire for recognition. The subject is therefore always driven by a structural imbalance. Ideological fantasms step in at the point where the subject in the symbolic order (language, law, the social) fails or lacks, and they offer a surrogate for the lost being. This happens through the creation of a scenario for

40   The Subject of Politics

what the Other desires, and thereby the answer to the question about what the subject must do in order to receive the recognition of the Other: finally an answer to the question of what the Other wants.

The answer fills out the empty place – the subject is bailed out from its eternal insecurity about what is the right thing to do, by identifying with the available descriptions and demands provided by the Other, which concern, for instance, the People, the Nation, the True Believers and their tasks. By thus containing a scenario of the complete and final recognition ('we will love you, if you act like this'), the fantasm points at a terrain beyond the metonymy, doubt and dissatisfaction of desire. Lacan uses the term 'jouissance', which is typically translated as 'enjoyment', to describe this fantasmatic condition of transcending the imperfect and provisional fulfilment in desire. Ideology offers us the imagination of being those who fulfil the desire of the Other – this is how we should be in order to be loved by the state, the leader, the *Führer*, God, etc.

Desire, however, *can* never be completely satisfied, and the lack of being can never be taken away. But the lack can be covered or explained, and this is precisely the function of the fantasm. In Nazism, for example, a fantasmatic conception of the Jew was created as the one who was hindering the German nation from developing its full potential. Through this construction it was possible to maintain the conviction that a particular 'German' essence existed that could be unfolded and lived out on condition of the elimination of the Jewish obstruction. Žižek writes the following about the use Nazis made of the figure of the Jew, which also makes it clear how Lacanian critique of ideology differs from discourse analytic approaches:

> [T]he 'criticism of ideology' consists in unmasking traditional allegory as an 'optical illusion' concealing the mechanism of modern allegory: the figure of the Jew as an allegory of Evil conceals the fact that it represents within the space of ideological narration the pre immanence of the textual operation that 'quilts' it. The real questions, however, are: How is this purely formal inversion possible? On what does it rely? More precisely: How is it possible that the result of a purely formal inversion acquires enough substantiality to be perceived as a

flesh-and-blood personality? The psychoanalytic answer is, of course, *enjoyment* – the only substance acknowledged by psychoanalysis, according to Lacan. (Žižek 1991a: 19)

As Žižek emphasises in several places, one does not overcome anti-Semitism by collecting and publishing facts about the Jews (they don't really want to undermine society or steal our women, money, etc.), but by investigating the role that the Jew plays in our own libidinal economy. It is not sufficient to show that the 'Jew' is a discursive construction. The critique of ideology must also display the enjoyment that maintains this construction. The critique of ideology must therefore be performed in two steps. The first is to show that a discursive order which gives an impression of being 'destined' or universal is really contingent and could have been different, and is building on a series of strategies through which the concrete ideological corpus has been created. The second step consists in showing how it isn't the factual, historical conditions that are the real basis or 'problem' of the discourse. On the contrary: behind the discursive strategies lies a structural and transhistorical necessity, namely the attempt in any ideological fantasm to cover or hide a traumatic lack.

> [I]deology is the exact opposite of internalization of external contingency: it resides in externalization of the result of an inner necessity, and the task of the critique of ideology here is precisely to discern the hidden necessity in what appears as a mere contingency. (Žižek 1994a: 4)

The task of critical theory is to examine the conditions of possibility for given, ideological configurations, and those structural dispositions that make possible, but do not determine, specific ideological appearances (Žižek 1993a: 2). What one could, although admittedly a little awkwardly, call the 'basis' in Žižek's system does not have the character of a societal matter from which the political ideas could be deduced, but rather has a (quasi) transcendental level – in this case the conditions of possibility for ideologically mediated identification. Here we reencounter the line of separation between the philosophical-transcendental level and the concrete, sociological level that can be extracted from Žižek's work: the philosophical analysis should articulate the preconditions, drives and interests in human existence – *why* we at all (need to) identify with ideological functions – while the sociological analysis should articulate these frames in their concrete materialisation – *which* ideologically mediated identities are actually at stake. The reading of Žižek is often complicated by the fact that these two levels are rarely kept apart.

The mirror stage as critique of ideology

Žižek has, to a large extent, developed his critique of ideology in a dialogue with the work of Louis Althusser, so in order to flesh this critique out a bit more we will first give a short description of the relation between Althusser and Lacanian psychoanalysis, and then articulate Žižek's criticism of Althusser.

Althusser opens his study of ideological state apparatuses by claiming that a social formation that does not reproduce the preconditions of its production would not last a year. Althusser's renewal of the Marxist tradition was to change the focus from production to reproduction, i.e. shifting from the analysis of the functioning of economy (production) to the analysis of the ruling ideology (capitalism) (Althusser 1984: 20). Althusser claims that while ideologies differ, they all share an 'eternal' status (ibid.: 33ff). This is due to the fact that ideologies will always form an integral part of society, since the subject represents its relation to society through ideological semantics. Ideology, for Althusser, is the precondition of any kind of identification. Ideology does not distort a societal reality, but creates an imaginary relation to a social formation, such that social reality can be presented.

Althusser does not write very extensively on the imaginary identification, so in order to spell it out a bit more we must address Lacan's text on 'The Mirror Stage as Formative of the Function of the I' (1977). In this text, it is Lacan's thesis that the child, between the ages of six and eighteen months, starts to see itself as an autonomous unity and is no longer entirely dependant on grown-ups. This image of itself is essential to the development of the child. By being reflected in the mirror image (its bodily imago), the child takes the shape of an 'I'.

This typically happens when the child literally sees itself in a mirror, or reflects itself in the care of its mother or other closely related persons. In the mirror, I see someone who looks exactly like me. The mirroring creates the imagination of a whole, autonomous subject – that looks like *this* – and which is thereby ready to take its role in the social matrix.

According to Althusser, however, the imaginary identification, understood as the subject's 'perception' of itself as an autonomous individual, tends to blind the subject to the constitutive character of the social surroundings, i.e. to the fact that the subject only takes the shape of an autonomous 'I' on the background of a symbolically mediated mandate. The precondition for symbolic identification, and thereby also for the function of ideologies, is that the subject can take the shape of an 'I' in order to constitute an experiencing centre. Without such a centre, the subject would not be able to fill out nor feel obligated by a particular subject position. On the other hand, the imaginary identification can only take place, if it is 'hooked on to' a symbolically interpellated mandate.

It is again important to emphasise that 'imaginary' does not mean fictive in the sense of false, but designates the ability to create and identify reflections. The 'symbolic' does not mean representations, but rather the moulds or structures that are the precondition for representation. Althusser expresses the double constitution of the subject in an imaginary and symbolic identification as follows: 'the category of the subject is constitutive of all ideology, but at the same time and immediately I add that *the category of the subject is only constitutive of all ideology insofar as all ideology has the function (which defines it) of "constituting" concrete individuals as subjects*' (Althusser 1984: 45).

Althusser develops the concept of interpellation to describe this double constitution. The term interpellation conceptualises an act and a challenge through which the subject is constituted as the subject of a symbolic calling. This can happen by someone literally addressing you, or by hearing the challenge, turning around, and believing that it was directed particularly at you. A classic example is the leader that addresses his subjects in the name of the fatherland, or the policeman who challenges you in the street. Interpellation thus conceptualises the illusion of having always already been a subject (ibid.: 46). The subject does not realise that it is constituted in the calling itself, and that this is therefore performative rather than ascertaining.

The subject's being blind to the constitutive character of the interpellation makes the ideological call appear as the declaration of truisms. Ideologies thereby have a naturalising function (ibid.: 49). Althusser, however, at this point seems to presuppose meaning to be a 'thing' that can be handed over in a way that makes it possible for the subject to be fully reflected in its symbolically interpellated mandate. The subject 'receives' his identity and a set of naturalised beliefs and becomes a subject by taking over this transportable ideological package, so to speak. Žižek, on the contrary, emphasises how the symbolic calling always misses its target. The subject feels interpellated, but this feeling is always accompanied by another feeling that could be paraphrased as a 'to do what?' or even just 'why?' The ideological call, in other words, is accompanied by a 'why me?' rather than a by an unproblematic mirroring of the subject. The symbolic remains external to the subject, and one could therefore claim that the subject has an inherent hysterical tendency (Žižek 1993a: 76–77). Why this mandate? Why me? It is as if something is missing. As the mirror image already illustrates, there is also a fundamental impossibility in a mirroring – one never really sees 'it all': something always misses out. If I see my face in a mirror, my neck escapes me, and so on. It is this impossibility that keeps haunting the subject. It is as if there is a hidden subjective core that is left untouched by the interpellation. Hysteria is another name for the impossibility of interpellation, and it is in the impossibility itself that subjectivity resides. Žižek writes on the hysterical subject:

> [T]he subject *does* always maintain a minimal of 'inner distance' towards the apparatuses and rituals in which ideology acquires material existence – his attitude towards this externality is always an 'I am not that' (my true self does not hinge on this stupid mechanism): ideological identification is always, as it were, an identification with fingers crossed... (Žižek 1996: 166)

The subject (mistakenly) holds on to the idea of there being a more truthful, complete core prior to the symbolic mandate: that 'I' still have, or am something in my core, that is at a distance from the 'me' that my family and society have appointed me to be. This does not mean that interpellations have no effect. On the contrary, postmodern ideologies exactly presuppose this kind of non-identification.

> Is not this hysterical distance towards interpellation, however, the very form of ideological misrecognition? Is not this apparent failure of interpellation, its self-relating disavowal ... *the ultimate proof of its success*, that is to say, of the fact that the 'effect-of-subject' really took place? And in so far as the Lacanian term for this innermost kernel of my being is *objet petit a*, is it not justifiable to claim that this *objet petit a*, the secret treasure, *agalma*, is the *sublime object of ideology* – the feeling that there is 'something in me more than myself' which cannot be reduced to any of my external symbolic determinations, that is, to what I am for others? Is not this feeling of an unfathomable and inexpressible 'depth' of my personality, this 'inner distance' towards what I am for others, the exemplary form of the *imaginary* distance towards the symbolic apparatus? Therein resides the crucial dimension of the ideological *effet-sujet*: not in my direct identification with the symbolic mandate ... but in my experience of the kernel of my Self as something which pre-exists the process of interpellation, as subjectivity *prior* to interpellation. (ibid.)

Althusser's concepts of 'interpellation' and 'subject position' seem to repeat some of the figures that he is criticising. He acknowledges that the essence of the subject is socially constructed, but the identity of the subject is still fully given in relation to the interpellations that it is prone to – which is also indicated by the term 'subject position'. Althusser seems to consider the subject as a whole and full being, with only one important difference to the theories of subjectivity and autonomy that he criticises: that this being is now socially constructed. He presupposes that the movement from the pre-ideological to the ideological has the character of a clean break and, accordingly, the acceptance of the interpellation will be total. The subject is absorbed by ideology. Žižek, on the contrary, claims that this process always leaves a remainder (Žižek 1989: 110). Not a remainder that escapes interpellation, but a remainder that emerges because of the impossibility of interpellation.

If one has a sociological temper, the question undoubtedly occurs of how society is possible and functions if the interpellations constantly miss their target. Žižek's reply is that it is possible because the social bond does not only consist in a positively valorised surface, but also in an obscene underside that activates the desire of the subject, or rather, gives it direction. Ideological fantasms cement society in the sense that they create a relation to common, desired objects. The fantasm in other words is a specific way of relating to a desired object. A particular object is sublimated qua the fantasm in a way that makes it appear as that which can heal the lack of being in the subject. This sublimated object has traditionally also, within psychoanalysis, been called a fetish. Let us pursue an elaboration of the work that a concept of fetishism may perform within the frame of the critique of ideology.

Fetishism as a political form

The object of desire, the '*objet petit a*', is only created in the subject's quest for it. More precisely, the *objet petit a* is the object-*cause* of desire in Lacanian terms, meaning that it is the fantasmatic object that one never fully 'gets', but which makes one constantly want *it*. The concrete, 'real' objects that one desires are therefore never completely it – although they can precisely be elevated or sublimated into playing the role, if you will, of the Object. The objects that have been made or have become sublime cannot therefore be confronted directly, since this would reveal them as ordinary objects without sublime qualities (Žižek 1991b: 12). The object is only sublime as long as we see it 'awry' – it is only sublime as long as it remains the embodiment of the (desired) small object a. Thus, the object is reduced to a simple, indifferent object when the fantasmatic frame disintegrates.

Hans Christian Andersen's *The Emperor's New Clothes* illustrates the problematic around the sublime object in a paradigmatic way. The emperor is fooled by two tailors into have a costume made for him that is so lavish and distinguished that only very bright people – like the emperor of course – can see it. Naïve and vain as the emperor is, he of course will not admit that he cannot see this amazing garment, and he therefore pretends and seems to convince everyone, even himself, that he does in fact see it. Or maybe more precisely: he seems to have convinced himself that *they*, his subjects, believe he can see it, and thereby that he must in fact be wearing it, since he is the emperor. According to Lacan, a madman who thinks that he is a king, emperor, Jesus, etc., is no crazier than a king who thinks that he is a king. A king, who thinks that he is a king, would be a king who identifies directly with his symbolic mandate (Žižek 1989: 25). The emperor in *The Emperor's New Clothes* is a fool, because he thinks that he, as the emperor, must be the wisest, most beautiful, most educated, etc., and therefore that he is 'naturally' the emperor – that his qualities and his office are directly and intimately connected. In the precise moment, however, when his subjects stop treating him as an emperor, he appears as merely one human among others. The emperor is the only one who ends up believing that he is wearing something; everyone else knows that he isn't. The central question therefore becomes why the subjects continue to treat him as the emperor. Andersen's story culminates on the day that the emperor shows his new garments to the public. Obviously, he is not in fact wearing anything, but no one dares mention it, until a little boy cries the (in)famous words: 'But he is not wearing anything!' The emperor hereafter appears as a fool, or more precisely: he no longer appears as emperor.

The classical reading of this act, in the critique of ideology, is to see it as a symbolic undressing of power. The emperor is just a simple human being when he is stripped of the attributes of power. This reading, however, is far too simple, since it merely uncovers the emperor as a product of his position in a social structure. The interesting point is not why the little boy symbolically undresses the emperor, but why everyone else doesn't. They can see that the emperor is not wearing anything – or can they? When they see the emperor as emperor, regardless of whether he is wearing anything or not, the reason of course is that they are seeing him 'awry'. They see the emperor as the incarnation of a sublime object, which makes him more than human. Thereby, they simultaneously overlook the fact that the emperor only becomes emperor in the moment they treat him as such. They overlook that the ritual, through which his body appears as a fetish, is creating the very social reality of which they are part, and that the emperor was nothing before and without the ritual practice (ibid.: 146f.).

Ernst Kantorowicz, in his study of medieval political theology, developed the thesis about the king's two bodies. The king has both a sublime ('political') and a natural body. As the incarnation of the kingdom, the king is immortal (which gives him a sublime body), while as a concrete individual he is of course mortal (which gives him a natural body). When the spectators don't undress the emperor in Hans Christian Andersen's fairy tale, it is precisely because he has two bodies – a natural and a sublime. The sublime body appears as a fantasmatic object of identification that makes the actual charisma appear in a special light. Details that we would find ordinary in other families suddenly become something special, because they are describing a royal family. Via the 'natural' body of the emperor, his subjects gain access to the sublime. There is something in the emperor more than the emperor, which means that what makes him an emperor is not the attributes of power – his placement in a social structure – but rather the emperor's function as a sublime, ideological object.

When the little boy's words cause such a stir, it is because he thereby strips the community of the object of its enjoyment. The boy's words not only have the effect of making the emperor appear ludicrous, they also cause the subject positions that were guaranteed by the emperor to disintegrate (Žižek 1994a: 58). The emperor's subjects don't 'see' the emperor as naked, but as the incarnation of a sublime body. This X in the emperor that is more than the emperor cannot be reduced to any physical object. One could also say that this object is the one that defines the emperor once all physical attributes have been taken away. Despite not wearing anything, the emperor still appeared as emperor.

The Emperor's New Clothes is thus a story that describes the problem of cynicism. If Marx in his theory of commodity fetishism wrote that 'they do not know it, but they are doing it', thereby viewing fetishism within the framework of a classical, modernist differentiation between essence and representation – between practice (commodity fetishism) and consciousness – Hans Christian Andersen's version must be: they know very well (that the emperor is not wearing anything), but still they are doing it (treating him like an emperor). In Lacanian terms, we know very well that the big Other does not exist, that the symbolic order is a fiction, but we obey nonetheless. The only thing the cynic believes in is enjoyment, and the symbolic order is only accepted because it serves as the condition of possibility for enjoyment, and because it thereby gives direction to desire.

It is, however, important to emphasise that this identification with the emperor is not a private matter. When I identify with the emperor, I first and foremost identify with the others who also identify with the emperor. When the little boy's words lead to disastrous consequences, it is not only because they reveal the emperor (the Other) as merely a product of the libidinal investments of his subjects, but also, in a last step, because the desublimation of the emperor's body disintegrates the bond between the emperor's subjects.

To recapitulate, the ideological fantasm can only function as long as the object is actually appearing as sublime. The object must therefore be found, bought, conquered, etc. It cannot appear as something that we simply 'make up'. One must believe that the fascination of the object stems from the object itself. The object must therefore be kept at a distance. If we come too near to it, like in the story about the emperor's new clothes, it is revealed to be only a common, ordinary object. Lacan, accordingly, defines anxiety not as the condition where you are afraid of losing the object, but on the contrary as produced by a too close contact with the object (Žižek 1991a: 8).

The two sides of the social bond

In the previous section, we argued that the subject does not subject itself to a hegemonic power on the background of purely discursive strategies. We know that the emperor is naked, but if we are cynical in relation to the law (the rules, values, norms... the social), then why obey? As already mentioned, it is because the law makes possible the imagination of something beyond the law – an individual being that escapes the law. This image, paradoxically, sustains the law. The transgression of the law is thereby already included in it.

Analytically, it can therefore be fruitful to maintain that the law has two sides – a surface and an underside: a surface consisting in written or unspoken prohibitions (norms, conventions, rules, etc.) and an underside permeated by enjoyment – a domain of transgression. Where the law prohibits enjoyment, the underside of the law communicates the opposite imperative: enjoy! The true master is unconscious; he is the one (qua superego), who demands enjoyment. No hegemony without a sub-current of fantasmatic enjoyment. There are two masters – a public, symbolic authority and a 'hidden', spectral master (a master behind the actually present master).

Perversion is therefore constitutive of the social field, and not something that violates or negates it. Nazism illustrates this better than anything. The pogroms of the night, the assaults on political opponents, were not destructive of the idyllic popular community. One could rather say that the precondition for an idyllic popular community is a brotherhood in guilt. Transgression in Nazism was not an individual phenomenon, but a socially constructed and ideologically valorised phenomenon.

> [O]ne can indulge in illicit drives, torture and kill for the protection of law and order, and so on. This perversion relies on the split of the field of Law into Law as 'Ego-ideal' – that is, symbolic order which regulates social life and maintains social peace – and into its obscene, superegotistical reserve. ... The deepest identification which 'holds a community together' is not so much identification with the Law which regulates its 'normal' everyday circuit as, rather, *identification with the specific form of transgression of the Law, of its suspension* (in psychological terms, with the specific form of enjoyment.) (Žižek 1992b: 225)

Žižek likes to tell military stories to illustrate this point. Isn't the repressed homosexuality in the army the best example? Here, we often find an explicit prohibition against homosexuality, while at the same time the jargon and a series of rituals are constructed around the transgression of this absolute prohibition. An often practised perverted 'practical joke' in the Yugoslavian army, while Žižek was doing his military service, was, for instance, to put one finger up the anus of the soldier waiting in front of you in the line at the mess, and then quickly turn away in order for the molested soldier not to register who did it. The perverted reappearance of homosexuality in stupid practical jokes thereby in reality sustained the explicit prohibition against homosexuality.

We can now specify the problem of cynicism a bit more closely. Cynicism 'disregards' the surface of the law and creates a distance to the symbolic mandates that it articulates. But the same cynicism maintains the underside of the law. It is the same subjects who are maintaining a cynical attitude towards the message of public ideology, who without any concerns participate in paranoid fantasies about conspiracies and about the enjoyment of the others (Žižek 1996: 142). This cynicism does not entail that the public ritual is without importance or that the ideological call is without effect and so on, but that it serves as a condition of possibility for enjoyment.

Awareness of the structuring of power, however, does give oppositional forces an interesting possibility of taking the official rhetoric 'too' literally. The acknowledgement that power is structured in an 'inconsistent' way around a fundamental inscrutability, and that it is resting on a fragile balance between civil and barbaric elements, can be used against power itself (ibid.: 3). The strategies that one could use in the struggle against totalitarian fantasms vary from situation to situation, but one thing seems to be clear: the classical strategy of exposure and enlightenment will often fall short in relation to an ideology that is legitimised through a cynical practice. One alternative strategy could instead be to pronounce the unspoken rules and thereby force the system in question to acknowledge their existence. By pronouncing these hidden rules, the system would be forced to react by either admissions or violence, and it would lose in either case (Helmer and Žižek 1995: 14ff). Žižek often refers to the rock and

52 The Subject of Politics

punk band Laibach to praise them for their ingenuity in this connection. Laibach's strategy was to over-identify with the obscene underside of the social bond and mix totalitarian symbols and slogans with perverse stage performance. The aim was to undermine the dominant social fantasms by making them explicit. Laibach's strategy:

> *'frustrates' the system (the ruling ideology) precisely in so far as it is not its ironic imitation, but overidentification with it* – by bringing to light the obscene superego underside of the system, overidentification suspends its efficiency. The ultimate expedient of Laibach is their deft manipulation of transference: their public (especially intellectuals) is obsessed with the 'desire of the Other' – What is Laibach's actual position? Are they truly totalitarians or not? – that is, they ask Laibach a question and expect an answer from them, failing to notice that Laibach themselves *function not as an answer but as a question*. (Žižek 1994b: 72)

To function as the question and not the answer is the task of the analyst in the psychoanalytic clinic. Laibach's strategy could also be said to be staging an aid for what Lacan calls 'traversing the fantasm'. In a clinical practice, this would mean that an analysand and an analyst meet on the basis of the analysand's expectation that the analyst is a subject that must know (what is wrong with the analysand). Roughly said, analysis starts by the analysand installing the analyst in the place of the big Other. The precondition for a successful (or any) analysis is thus a transference (of expectation, trust, love) between the two involved parties. This transference is a necessary condition for analysis to get started, but it also quickly becomes a problem.

The purpose of analysis is, in one interpretation, to acknowledge that the big Other doesn't exist – that there is no (hidden) truth about the subject, and that it must therefore take responsibility for itself and its own existential project. Traversing the fantasm would not mean to dissolve it, though, but analysis could result in basing it or relating to it differently. Is this not precisely the strategy that Laibach was employing? Analysis ideally allows us to recognise that the negativity that, for instance, is projected onto the figure of the Jew (or whoever takes the Jew's place), is really only an expression of a fundamental lack in the desiring subject itself. One must identify with one's symptom in order to ameliorate one's condition, i.e., *in casu*, one must identify with the Jew as the excess which is telling a truth about oneself (Žižek 1989: 128).

In other words, the task of the critique of ideology consists in letting us undergo a specific kind of analysis: it forces us to traverse the fantasm in order to realise how some of the most libidinally invested imaginations we have are projections of the wish to have desire fulfilled through a particular object – either in its 'actual' fulfilment (the emperor, the idol), or as that which precludes fulfilment (the Jew, the Muslim, the EU, the unemployed, the criminal, etc.). Identifying with the symptom means acknowledging one's own gaze inscribed into the image of the other. The question is in all cases directed back to the subject. The end of analysis is the fall of the big Other, i.e. giving up on the fantasy of an inscrutable connection between everything that the Other wants to maintain and which defines the subject's place.

Chapter 3. A world out of joint: Žižek's diagnosis of contemporary society

After the structural description of ideology and after placing Žižek in the landscape of the critique of ideology, we will now move to more direct analyses of contemporary political issues: Žižek's diagnosis of contemporary society. After having been among the most prominent voices in the Slovene opposition in the years leading to national independence and the first presidential election in 1990, Žižek quickly became a recognised analyst of what one could call the decline, if not disappearance, of politics, i.e. the perception that the dissolution of the Soviet Union and 'really existing socialism' heralded the final overcoming of the struggle between ideologies to the benefit of (ideologically neutral) liberal democracy, and the mainly administrative management of citizens' interests in the countries where democracy already prevails – a perception that was of course famously manifested in Francis Fukuyama's book *The End of History and the Last Man* in 1992. Žižek shares the analysis that in a significant sense we are living after an epoch where political systems failed massively, but he does not accept that this means that we have to abandon radical politics as such. What this entails, we shall return to in chapter 4. First, we will take a closer look at some of the elements in the more detailed analysis of contemporary society that Žižek offers.

Žižek does not share the optimism or celebration of the fact that 'the grand narratives' can no longer be told, as it is commonly expressed of the postmodern condition. The accompanying understanding that we are now finally free to live our lives as we ourselves prefer is also a truth that begs for more scrutiny. In a sense, Žižek is in fact radically pessimistic, to the degree that one could almost quote Voltaire's revolted poem after the earthquake in Lisbon in 1755: 'Come, ye philosophers, who cry "All's well", and contemplate this ruin of a world'. Voltaire was revolting against rationalist philosophical attempts at justifying evils as necessary by-products in the 'best of all possible words', while Žižek could be said to be doing something comparable against the idea of having reached the best of all possible political systems. The world's problems in terms of wars, persecution, hunger, environmental degradation and so on, have certainly not been solved by the declaration of victory for liberal capitalist democracy. On the other hand, Žižek does not share the *theoretical* pessimism that there is nothing more to say because a new and final world order has been established and there is no new, grand project to realise. Žižek's project could be said to be keeping the possibility open for a new, radical and future oriented political engagement in philosophy, social theory, etc., through the analysis of the current human mode of existence. We must 'traverse the fantasy', i.e. confront the unacknowledged implications of our own actions, and the purpose must be to reach a new beginning and to nourish a political creativity that points beyond the current states of affairs. In Lacanian terms, this process could more precisely be compared to *La Passe* – the passage from the position of analysand to that of analyst. The passage from being held captured by certain, pathological patterns of behaviour to a position or a perspective that allows one to (re)interpret.

The fall of the Father

In Mark Joffe's 2001 film *The Man Who Sued God*, a story is told that can serve as a rough frame for the understanding of Žižek's diagnosis of our time. The film is about a fisherman and former lawyer, Steve Myers, whose boat is struck by lightning and destroyed. When Myers wants to cash his expected coverage from the insurance company he is told that the insurance does not cover an 'act of God', i.e. entirely unforeseeable accidents where ordinary conditions do not apply. Instead of accepting the rejection, however, Myers decides that someone must be made responsible and pay him compensation, and since the accident was allegedly an 'act of God', it must be God himself who should be put on trial (which then happens via His representatives on this side). Leaving aside the fact that the movie is rather mediocre, the plot does illustrate that the postmodern human being in its supposedly free and careless existence still needs some authority to hold responsible for the inscrutable dimensions of life or its entirely unexpected suffering. Paradoxically, in an historical epoch where humanity should be on its way towards greater independence and autonomy for all, authorities are as much in demand as ever. An analysis that only focuses on formal and institutional limitations in the self-realisation of individuals will not be able to acknowledge this perspective.

In much the same way, the conception of postmodern identity formation as a narrating individuality is only correct insofar as it includes into the picture the necessarily accompanying idea of an authority that limits, disturbs, or (thereby) legitimises the individual narration. It might be true that the System has fallen – that there is no longer any divine law or even a set political framework that prescribes what every individual should do – but nonetheless the System still functions. The big Other does not exist, but it functions nonetheless. We would rather maintain that the Other wants something specific from us, than take on ourselves the 'abyss of freedom' in having to articulate our own lives without restrictions. *The Man Who Sued God* illustrates this condition by its ironic insistence on a divine guarantor behind something as profane as an insurance policy, or on an ultimate complaints board to which the human being can direct its complaint in as far as it cannot handle its own situation (Žižek 2003: 169). As a metaphor for postmodern society, the film therefore illustrates the 'culture of complaint'. Instead of embracing the freedom that opened up as a matter of fact with the collapse of the brutal political experiments of the twentieth century, the postmodern subject is clinging to the idea of an authority that can be blamed for the state of things.

A similar paradox is known within psychoanalysis as the problem that the patient, after completed treatment, i.e. after having become able to interpret his or her symptoms, still clings on to them. Žižek illustrates this paradox with the joke about the man who thought that he was a corn. The man-corn was hospitalised in a psychiatric hospital, because his conviction led to paranoia of being eaten by a chicken. The man was cured and discharged, but after only a short while he came running back and wanted to be let in again. The doctor asked him in surprise: 'Why are you coming back? You are cured; you know very well that you are not a corn'. 'Yes, yes,' the man replied, 'but does the *chicken* know?' (Žižek 1999: 325–6).

The original optimism in Freud's analytical project contained a kind of naivety, because it was assumed that the problem was 'only' to find the explanation for the symptom, i.e. to 'solve the rebus' which the symptom represented to the analysand. Once the pieces of the puzzle were put together and it was clear to the analysand wherein the pathological behaviour had its origin, the symptom would disappear – it would have been interpreted away. Clinical practice, however, demonstrates that this optimism is not always corroborated by the results. Even though the symptom is placed in a coherent and meaningful frame of interpretation, the analysand maintains his or her behaviour – clinging to the symptom. ('I know very well that I am only postponing the finalisation of my project because of an irrational fear of what is there on the other side'; 'I know very well that my paranoia is really a fantasy construction of my own', etc., 'but nonetheless I am doing it'.) Why is that?

The end of analysis as the fall of the big Other means the realisation of the fact that there was no big, coherent story with an inscrutable giver of the law, a father figure or a secret wirepuller who was causing my neurotic reactions, for example. It was me, myself, who created them all along. (The assumption that one 'chooses one's own neuroses' is fundamental to psychoanalysis and gives a rather strict aim of making the analysand responsible for his or her own character and action, contrary to some popular perceptions of psychoanalysis (Zupančič 2000: 35)). The problem in this definition is that it heralds a very risky condition for the patient. If there is no secret behind it all, does this mean that it is my own responsibility to make everything work? Am I responsible for everything that happens to me?

Put in another way, and seen from the perspective of the child: even though it may appear as a great liberation and as reaching a level of equity to reveal that one's father doesn't know 'it' either, when his impotence is finally revealed in the questions that he can no longer answer (the child's eagerness to ask – why this and why that – is not only an expression of curiosity, but just as much of a search for the limitations of the father figure) – it may just as well result in radical insecurity and anxiety. If the father/analyst does not know it, then who does? The risk is that this realisation can end in an actual psychotic breakdown, and this is why we prefer to let the big Other function even though we know that it doesn't exist. It is a very unsafe condition to be in when there is no longer an Other to refer to, and therefore the disposition to sustain its function is a powerful force. It is this structure that Žižek rediscovers in the postmodern relation to authority.

> [F]ar from cheerfully assuming the nonexistence of the big Other, the subject blames the Other for its failure and/ or impotence, as if *the Other is guilty of the fact that it doesn't exist*, that is, as if impotence is no excuse – the big Other is responsible for the very fact that it wasn't able to do anything: the more the subject's structure is 'narcissistic', the more he puts the blame on the big Other, and thus asserts his dependence on it. (Žižek 1999: 361)

We thereby encounter Lacan's reversal of Dostoyevsky's famous dictum that when God is dead, everything is allowed: when God is dead, *nothing* is allowed. He is therefore allowed to reign, even though he no longer exists. Without an authority to address its demands to, the subject has no frame for its narration and thereby no power in relation to which it can define itself. The unconscious trade-off between the ideological state apparatus and the interpellated subject is thus that the subject 'promises' not to fight for any change, while it, in return, is allowed to enjoy its status as a law abiding citizen, including the obscene underside that was described above. Even though there is no real manipulator or mastermind behind it all, and thereby no actual or declared contract between the agents, the 'deal' is implicitly acknowledged in a number of contexts. Political and marketing strategies can often benefit from aiming at giving the subject a sense of there being a call or an expectation that it has to live up to, or that it is possible to find a stable identity in a political movement or a commodity that answers the subject's insecurity. A good example of such strategies is a slogan from the biggest Danish bank, *Danske Bank*, that says 'Do what you are best at', i.e. don't worry about the end of the great narratives, the future of the globe, or the hunger in Africa, just do what you are good at, whether it be dancing or fishing, and let the Father/Leader/System take care of the overall questions. Žižek would have added that one can almost hear an accompanying 'And enjoy it!' Authority today is exercised through imperatives of enjoyment, self-realisation and extreme experiences.

Žižek's claim is that the fine balance between the authority displayed openly in the shape of the law and the one that finds expression in obscene lures, has been displaced in favour of the latter. The big Other functions unconsciously through our clinging on to the idea of an institution, authority or a community that demands something from the individual subject. The imperative of enjoyment (in the name of the big Other) is a form of self-interpellation. The superego does not function as a repetition of the explicit prohibitions in the law, but on the contrary as a silent injunction. By realising ourselves, enjoying life, etc., we simultaneously confirm our position in the symbolic order, and thereby that it works. It can be very stressful to enjoy life so intensely: every man must have a successful career, a fantastic sex life, do the proper jogging, take care of his body, be a good father and a considerate husband, have interesting hobbies and go on interesting holidays, etc., etc. The confirmation of enjoyment itself becomes the actual target, and we therefore also see more and more products that contain the imaginary enjoyment-value without their original malignant content: coffee without caffeine, beer without alcohol, butter without fat, and so on. In other words: enjoyment without enjoyment.

The right combination of moderation and excessive enjoyment can be an effective political engine. As Nietzsche noticed, asceticism is often accompanied by 'orgies of feelings', i.e. a sublime sense of self in the individual that torments itself by refraining from indulging in (immediate) sensual pleasure. Something similar is going on in the enjoyment without enjoyment: by creating the impression that we are the ones who make society function, we are also able to frame an idea of those who enjoy at our expense: the unemployed, the criminal, the coloured or the foreigners. There is thus Lacanian *jouissance* at stake in the modest restraint towards pleasure. While we consider ourselves to be hard working, humble subjects refraining from laziness, drunkenness, adultery, etc., we shamelessly enjoy being those that thereby fulfil the unspoken demands of the Other. Enjoyment is therefore at stake in two different levels that should more precisely be differentiated as pleasure and enjoyment, respectively. Nietzsche's description of asceticism as orgies of feelings relates to the *enjoyment* in the voluntary abstinence from *pleasure*. Enjoyment without enjoyment is thus enjoyment without pleasure.

So, not only do we create a particular form of self-interpellation, we also (thereby) construe the Other's demand to us: through self-interpellation the Other is staged, as well as the Other's desire. Self-interpellation gives us an (imagined) answer to the question: 'What does the Other want from me?' In a series of articles, Žižek has attempted to capture various contemporary ways in which the self-sacrificing, decent subject is construed in opposition to a subject supposed to relish in immediate looting, fornication, rape, drinking, etc. For instance, the reports about widespread looting and rape in New Orleans after Hurricane Katrina in 2005 later appeared to have been vastly exaggerated. In the days after the natural disaster, numerous news reports appeared about how black people in particular were raging through the streets, but when the storm (including the one in the media) had settled, it appeared that a great number of these stories were actually based on quickly emerging urban legends.

Why were these stories so significantly exaggerated and so quickly and uncritically distributed? It was because they confirmed the expectation of ordinary, 'righteous' people that someone else was doing that which they themselves were heroically abstaining from. This confirmation was the real driving force behind the stories, and it was therefore not even of crucial importance to Žižek that many of them simply turned out to be false. Much like Jacques Lacan's claim that a jealous husband had to be considered as a patient with a pathological condition, even though his wife did in fact engage in extra-marital affairs, so this instantaneous reassurance in the media (regardless of whether it had been 'corroborated' by more factual evidence) was an expression of the self-interpellation in the economy of enjoyment.

> *[E]ven if ALL reports of violence and rape were to be proved factually true, the stories circulating about them would still be 'pathological' and racist*, since what motivated these stories was not facts, but racist prejudices, the satisfaction felt by those who would be able to say: 'You see, blacks are really like that, violent barbarians under the thin layer of civilisation!' In other words, we would be dealing with what one can call *lying in the guise of truth*: even if what I am saying is factually true, the motives that make me say it are false. (Žižek 2008: 85)

Nationalism and ethnic conflicts

Underneath the surface of the economy of enjoyment, the danger of a radical experience of a loss of reality is always present. The so called network society that we live in contains a threat of appearing as a dematerialised reality without substance and without firm reference points. Therefore, this society fosters a strong wish for safety and new points of reference in replacement of the ones that disappeared. Even though the ideological self-interpellation is quite an effective political and economical engine on the level of the symbolic and the imaginary, the subject is left with an unclear sense that something is missing – that there must be a real level, a background or substance more real than the one we experience directly, and which conditions the order that we are part of. This longing for the real is not necessarily a longing for a negation of the network society as it functions today, but much rather its necessary supplement. We partake in a complex game of identification processes, but is there a real core to all this, a kind of extremity or kernel that anchors our self-perception? We are longing, you could say, to meet ourselves – our real selves – and not just the dull, everyday replica of a self that we meet in the office or in the bosom of the family.

Extreme sports are an example of how this longing is materialised in postmodern society after the fall of the Father: we seek an extremity to confirm that we are 'really' more than our everyday existence and thereby that it is in fact 'well founded'. Another example could be the so called 'cutters', and especially the teenage girls who cut themselves for no apparent reason. Often, these girls have a hard time explaining what it is they wish to achieve by maiming themselves. Mostly, there is in fact no strong death wish, for example, but rather a wish to find a kind of evidence of being alive – something more real to measure life by. The chaotic modern world that presents itself to them does not give 'enough' identification in the pre-established roles available to them and which they are expected to play. Therefore, they must seek more drastic measures.

Is not the logic behind strong nationalist tendencies the same? By 'cutting in ourselves', i.e. going a level deeper down into our identity, we expect to find a more original substance that gives meaning and direction to an otherwise confused and fragmented life. In this way, phenomena like ethnic conflict, hooliganism and hate crimes can even be seen as 'necessary' supplements to the network society. The purpose of nationalist rhetoric does not have to be to overturn society, redistribute goods and welfare, etc.; on the contrary: it is most often exactly the consolidation of existing society that is the purpose, and this is achieved by rooting it in a set of ideas about culture, traditions, holy places, buildings, etc. Everything remains the same, but it suddenly makes sense: it is like this, because we are like this.

The identity thus construed is of course much easier to manifest if it stands in a clear relation to something it is not, and this is why the 'eternal Jew' is always relevant as that which blocks our harmonic identity. In the book *Tarrying with the Negative* from 1993 – written at a time when the dissolution of Yugoslavia was still in a very critical phase – Žižek defines that which the foreigners, enemies, others, are trying to steal from us as the 'Nation-Thing', i.e. a sublime kernel that defines us – fills out the 'empty place', covers the inherent lack in our social and political reality – and which only gets its true signification once it is considered to be threatened:

> What we conceal by imputing to the Other the theft of enjoyment is the traumatic fact that we never possessed what was

allegedly stolen from us: the lack ('castration') is originary, enjoyment constitutes itself as 'stolen'. (Žižek 1993a: 203)

It is thus the loss of the loss which represents the real danger to the nationalist subject: having to admit that the lost golden past is an ideological fantasy. A perfect example of this is of course the Serbian investment in the legend of the defeat to the Turks on the *Kosovo Polje* in 1389. The battle was real enough, but the almost mythological significance it has acquired is difficult to understand without an analysis of the enjoyment and fantasies it has fostered. Slobodan Milosevič' famous speech on the 600th anniversary of the battle (in front of a million Serbs) is usually interpreted as the beginning of the end of Yugoslavia and the initiation of the violent ethnic conflicts of the following years (i.e. from 1989–1994). It was in 1389 that the 'loss' occurred – since then, the Serbian nation had allegedly been persecuted and humiliated – and now the Kosovo Albanians were threatening to steal this loss, i.e. to tear this birthplace with mythological significance of a people with a glorious and lost past, away from Serbia. The Serbs were indeed easier to address as a people when they were facing enemies that threatened to take away their traumatic heritage. Soon after, a series of 'precautionary measures' could be directed at the Albanian population, while the Serbian minorities in Croatia and Bosnia in particular were also more directly addressed from Belgrade. It is not difficult to apply the same logic to the original Germanic, or Arian, nation that was threatened by the Jews, or even to the economies of enjoyment in contemporary Western countries where populist rightwing parties are also making their voices count.

> This shift in the Zeitgeist is where real danger lurks: it prepares the ground for the possible hegemony of an ideology which perceives the presence of 'aliens' as a threat to national identity, as the principal cause of antagonisms that divide the political body. (Žižek 1993b: 233)

However, things are, as always, not that simple for Žižek. If one could only identify the upcoming nationalist emotions among Slovenes, Croats, Serbs, etc., after the collapse of the Yugoslavian system as the unitary cause of the wars and bloodshed in Croatia, Bosnia, and Kosovo, then things would be intellectually easy to handle. But there is one factor in these clashes that is usually given too little attention: the influence of the Western world and its 'gaze' on the ethnic conflicts in former Yugoslavia. As Rado Riha has written, the European gaze identified being Slovene, Croat, Serb, or, in short, 'Yugoslavian', with 'Being-Nationalist' much too quickly (Riha 1993: 22). In the mostly peaceful revolutions in Eastern Europe, Western Europeans had been able to see themselves reflected in the image of populations that had strong wishes of establishing new liberal, capitalist democracies, but in the former Yugoslavian republics the image was more blurred. From the point of view of Northern and Western Europe, what in the Balkans was, to a large degree, considered as struggles for independence and autonomy, was perceived as a release of archaic nationalist violence that had been kept at bay by the strict rule of former president Tito.

The tragedy is that the perception of the Yugoslavian peoples as particularly obsessed by their nationalist-being contributed to *creating* the nationalist violence that actually caused havoc in the region. The peace negotiations and attempts at mediation that the Western powers took part in were too much compromised by the inscription of this gaze into the understanding of what the conflicts were about. Žižek compares the European and American arbiters around 1990 with the ethnographical expedition that went to New Zealand to investigate the rumour that a local tribe was dancing a particularly terrific war dance in grotesque death masques. When the expedition had reached its destination late one night in a remote village, the ethnographers asked if they could witness the dance, and the next day, their wish was granted. The ethnographers went home satisfied and wrote a report that received much praise. Unfortunately, it was later discovered that the dance was only performed – it was *invented* – in order to try and meet the request that the expedition had asked. The 'natives' had been sitting up all night to come up with a dance that they thought might fit the expectations of their unexpected visitors (Žižek 1993b: 237). In a similar way, the Yugoslavian wars were to some extent 'performed' as a result of a more or less explicit expectation among Western powers to see such an outcome of the liberation of the Balkanised subject.

> Far from being the Other of Europe, former Yugoslavia was rather Europe itself in its Otherness, the screen onto which Europe projected its own repressed reverse. (ibid.: 238)

The general point in all these examples is Hegelian, namely that the gaze is inscribed into that which is gazed at: the alien that (is considered as the one who) wants to steal our intimate essence is covering our own inconsistent identity; the democratic enthusiasm in the former socialist countries in Eastern Europe confirmed the Western countries in an enthusiasm that we had forgotten (and allowed us to recognise ourselves through the others as democratic, peaceful, free, etc.); the expectation of 'archaic ethnic violence' in the Balkans exonerated Western Europe and the US from any responsibility for the violent development in the dissolution of Yugoslavia.

Multiculturalism and racism

One reaction to the violent ethnic conflicts of the twentieth century has been so-called 'multiculturalism'. Its ambition is explicitly to create a political culture of peaceful coexistence between different cultural and ethnic groupings. The keyword in these efforts is of course recognition. By recognising the existence of cultural differences we may create a harmonic unity of otherwise internally inconsistent traditions and convictions. The citizens of a state must first of all recognise each other's right to difference, i.e. that we do not necessarily have to understand each other or want anything from each other, but we must respect each other. Žižek spends more time criticising this conviction than on criticising nationalism, which makes sense in the light of what was established in the preceding chapter: the need to expose the secret, unacknowledged underside of liberal democracy. Multiculturalism, in this perspective, turns out to be a form of racism – and maybe an even more dangerous form than the one which is openly admitted.

As one of the most prominent spokesmen of multiculturalism, Will

Kymlicka himself acknowledges, multiculturalism shares a number of its basic conceptualisations with racism (Kymlicka 1995: 6). This is because multiculturalism defines a group of citizens in terms of their membership of the group, i.e. because of their origin or cultural heritage. Belonging to the group alone justifies that its members have certain rights that non-members do not have (regarding religious holidays, access to and ownership of land, and so on), while non-members may have rights that do not apply to the members (mostly because of the group's own internal restrictions in the shape of sexual taboos, prohibition against alcohol, choice of spouse, and so on). Žižek's critique of multiculturalism has two elements: partly, the common traits between multiculturalism and racism are more than just superficial; and partly, the cultural turn in its obsession with ethnicity, origin, etc., blurs the fact that our societies are still capitalist, and it thereby represents a denial of fundamental issues of distribution, exploitation, alienation, etc.

> It is in fact as if, since the horizon of social imagination no longer allows us to entertain the idea of an eventual demise of capitalism – since, as we might put it, everybody tacitly accepts that *capitalism is here to stay* – critical energy has found a substitute outlet in fighting for cultural differences which leave the basic homogeneity of the capitalist world-system intact. (Žižek 1999: 218)

Let us begin with the first part of the diagnosis. The transition from what one could call the superficial (as Kymlicka claims) to a deeper concordance between multiculturalism and racism happens when multiculturalism goes from partaking in a struggle against chauvinistically motivated discrimination to becoming a struggle for general group-rights *as* the struggle for individual rights. When membership of a minority becomes a politically relevant (or rather: *the* politically relevant) consideration, multiculturalism is no longer innocent. Sometimes this engenders almost absurd consequences, like when Iris Young claimed that all of the following groups in American society should be granted political representation as minorities: women, blacks, Native Americans, chicanos, Puerto Ricans and other Spanish speaking Americans, gays, lesbians, workers, poor people, old people and mentally and physically disabled people (Young 1989: 261). Any individual belongs to a group through which it brings forward its demands of recognition and rights. Often, this results in demands which the state simply cannot meet, and thereby group identities become identified as those who are discriminated in *this* particular way (cf. the complaint against the impotence/inexistence of the big Other).

This tendency has been vividly described in Robert Hughes' *The Culture of Complaint* (Hughes 1993): post-political identity construction often consists in a narrative structure where an individual or a group understands themselves as those who are suffering or who are obstructed in their own particular way. Multiculturalism can in this way, again in Žižekian, legitimise the subject's attachment to the group in a double sense: partly as subjected to the group's traditions and norms, partly as 'stuck' in an identity that is in contrast to and potentially threatened by others outside the group. In its pure form, multiculturalism simply corroborates the perception that the world is divided into groups that should live separately and not get in each other's way. 'Apartheid is thus legitimized as the ultimate form of anti-racism, as an endeavour to prevent racial tensions and conflicts' (Žižek 1993b: 224).

More moderately expressed, the focus on the common good is somewhat weakened in multiculturalism, as well as the focus on the ability to break with received patterns of behaviour and create new alliances across cultural and religious divides. A multiculturalist keeps the other at a distance and simultaneously, like the nationalist, uses the other as a measure for his or her own identity: by understanding, tolerating and recognising the other, the multiculturalist sustains him or herself as the excellent individual who is fundamentally understanding, tolerant, etc. Multiculturalism is a racism, because it confirms its own ethical distinctions by keeping the other at a distance through 'understanding' it.

> The fascinating 'diversity' of the Other functions as a fetish by means of which we are able to preserve the unproblematic *identity* of ours subjective position: although we pretend

> to 'historically relativize' our position, we actually conceal its split. ... To 'understand the Other' means to pacify it, to prevent the meeting with the Other from becoming a meeting with the Real that undermines our own position. (Žižek 1991a: 102)

It is as if the respect for the other is in reality motivated by a wish to manifest one's own stable and neutral position. This wish is sometimes expressed in slips and unconscious mistakes. A remarkable example from Denmark is the ever more widespread use of the word 'ethnic' as something that designates people who are not ethnic *Danes*. You often hear about introductions of bills in parliament concerning 'ethnic youths', many people like to shop in 'ethnic shops' (meaning shops owned by immigrants), etc. Regardless of the often respectful tone, this use of the word is obviously meaningless and/or in reality racist, since describing a broad multiplicity of people as 'ethnic' in contrast to an imagined neutral nucleus of blond Danes without ethnicity presupposes an empty signifier – a subject without being or identity. 'Ethnos' means people or culture, and one must therefore be ethnic-something, whether it be Turkish or Danish. The canonisation of the meaningless and/or unintended racist way of handling the linguistic challenges of multicultural society occurred in Denmark in 2005 with the establishment of nothing less than the 'Rehabilitation Centre for Ethnic Women in Denmark'. The name itself displays a 'knowledge that does not know itself' (cf. chapter 1).

The other element in Žižek's critique of multiculturalism is, as mentioned, that it blurs more fundamental political questions. In an important sense it is an extension of the post-political liberal-capitalist world order, where diversity, multiplicity, freedom and self-expression are highly appreciated *on condition that the most basic political order is not brought into question*. The tolerance in multiculturalism, therefore, paradoxically only recognises the other as long as he or she remains the same as us. When the other is really different from us, like in questions of circumcision, women's place in the family, religious prohibitions, or in radical political demands, tolerance ceases. Why was the whole world upset about the Taleban's 'barbaric' destruction of the gigantic Buddha-statues in Afghanistan?

Wasn't it exactly a straightforward consequence of the Islamic prohibition against depicting the Creation (and especially living creatures with some relation to the Divine)? In a way, the outrage of the situation was simply that the Taleban actually *believed* what they believed.

In Denmark a comparable problematic, though with almost 'inverted' roles, was seen in 2005–6. The country's biggest daily, *Jyllands-Posten*, published 12 suggestions as to what the Prophet Muhammad might have looked like. (The editor had asked cartoonists to draw 'Muhammad as you see him'). One of the drawings depictured Mohammed with a turban and a bomb, more than indicating that the cartoonist 'saw' the Prophet as a terrorist. This of course offended most of the Muslim minority in Denmark, and it created widespread protests and boycotts in a number of Muslim countries. In Denmark, public debates about freedom of speech, self-censorship, and the role of the media issued in the aftermath of the publication of the cartoons, and of course for good reasons. However, a debate about the actual issue in the conflict was almost completely absent: why a prohibition against depicturing the Prophet? Could there be good reasons for such a stance? The reaction among non-Muslim Danes (i.e. the Danes that are not 'ethnic'…) was rather to increase the distance to that which makes the other *other*: religion should remain a private matter and should not be articulated in public. The otherness of the other should remain hidden. We 'respect' you, but we don't understand you, i.e. we will leave you alone as long as you keep your emotions, etc. to yourself. In an article for the New York Times in March 2006, Slavoj Žižek claimed that the true friends of the Muslim minorities in Europe are, paradoxically enough, the 'true atheists' who will not refrain from discussing anything with anyone: 'While a true atheist has no need to boost his own stance by provoking believers with blasphemy, he also refuses to reduce the problem of the Muhammad caricatures to one of respect for other's beliefs' (Žižek 2006).

The predominant multiculturalist politeness on the other hand keeps the other at a safe distance and lets him believe whatever he wants, as long as it has no consequences for others, i.e. as long as it does not disturb the secular, post-political, capitalist world market system. Multiculturalism thereby legitimises the conviction that there are no longer any genuine political questions, and that the current order is 'politically neutral'. There is no longer any war, only large scale police actions where terrorists are being fought. There is no longer any exploitation – only unforeseen and provisional effects of the slow adaptation of third world countries to free market economy. There is no longer any class struggle – only administrative initiatives to encourage people to take jobs, etc. In terms of Žižek's 2008 book on violence, we have grown blind to the 'objective' or 'systemic' violence, the one inherent in the global economical and political systems, and instead focus only on 'subjective' violence – violence with a clear subject behind the act that harasses, steals, loots, rapes, etc. It is as if there are no longer any universal moral or political questions, only local incidents of subjective violence within a neutral, administrative setting. This is simultaneously why Žižek prefers Pope John Paul II to the Dalai Lama:

> One can now understand why the Dalai Lama is much more appropriate for our postmodern permissive times: he presents us with a vague feel-good spiritualism without any *specific* obligations: anyone, even the most decadent Hollywood star, can follow him while continuing his or her money-grabbing promiscuous lifestyle... The Pope, in contrast, reminds us that there *is* a price to pay for a proper ethical attitude – it is his very stubborn clinging to 'old values', his ignoring the 'realistic' demands of our time even when the arguments seem 'obvious' (as in the case of the raped nun), that makes him an authentic ethical figure. (Žižek 2001a: 181)

When John Paul caused a stir, it was in fact because he, like the Taleban, insisted on 'paying the price', i.e. on maintaining the prohibition against condoms, abortion, etc., even though all the liberals in the world cried out against it as old fashioned and intolerant. The Western Buddhists (inspired by the Dalai Lama), on the other hand, imagine themselves to be endlessly innocent, because their 'religiosity' can be practiced with a few candles at home in the evening, while the outside world is raging on with war, exploitation, social exclusion, etc. (We shall return to the relation between multiculturalism/ postmodernism and capitalism in chapter 4).

Žižek insists that the leftwing must wake up and rediscover that a political engagement is not innocent. There is no non-violent achievement of a just order of society, as long as the prevailing order is sustained by raw power, suppression, and 'objective violence'. The paradox is that such a view is often today seen as totalitarian and cynical or mean, while at the very same time a quite similar reasoning is accepted as legitimising Western hegemonic intervention around the world.

Terrorism and 11 September

The metaphor of 'waking up' was used frequently to describe the reaction in American society after the terror attacks of 11 September 2001. They were a 'wake up call', as it was often termed: we should not kid ourselves – there are people out there who want us dead, and we should focus on them, rather than on petty local problems like health reform, budget deficits, etc. As often before, Žižek's point was exactly the opposite: the attacks finally allowed the Americans to fall asleep again. After having been tormented by bad conscience and a form of international realism since the Vietnam War, 9-11 allowed the USA to finally put the traumatic immediate past behind itself and confirm the old role as innocent defender of world peace and (universal) 'American' values. The shock that most people saw as unreal or as something that we would never have thought possible, was at the same time what America 'needed' to fall asleep again. It was the realisation of what it had been fantasising about already for several years. Take a look at films like *Escape from New York*, *Independence Day* or *Fight Club* to confirm this theory. (The last of the three actually ends with the bombing and collapse of a number of the central buildings in the American economic system).

Just four days after the attacks on the World Trade Centre and the Pentagon, Žižek published an article with the first version of what later became the book *Welcome to the Desert of the Real*. The title is a quotation from the Wachowski-brothers' film *The Matrix* from 1999, which presents a radically scepticist scenario. The material reality that we all experience and see around us, is in fact virtual, generated and coordinated by a gigantic computer to which we are all attached. When the film's hero, Neo, has finally escaped from the computer simulated reality to the gloomy real world outside (the remnants of a global war that humans lost), he is received by Morpheus with the words: 'Welcome to the desert of the real'. The comparison with the situation of the USA and most of the Western world after 9-11 lies nearby. As Žižek wrote immediately after the catastrophe:

> It is precisely now, when we are dealing with the raw *Real* of a catastrophe, that we should bear in mind the ideological and fantasmatic coordinates which determine its perception. IF there is any symbolism in the collapse of the WTC towers, it is not so much the old-fashioned notion of the 'center of financial capitalism,' but, rather, the notion that the two WTC towers stood for the center of the VIRTUAL capitalism, of financial speculations disconnected from the sphere of material production. The shattering impact of the bombings can be accounted for only against the background of the borderline which today separates the digitalized First World form the Third World 'desert of the Real'. (Žižek 2001b: 2)

One could therefore interpret the attacks of 11 September quite literally as 'the return of the Real': the increasingly virtual economy was reminded of the real, material reality outside it. While we were convincing ourselves and each other that the working class had disappeared, dirty, badly paid and very manual labour was still being done in China and third world countries, as it is today. Bill Gates' utopian idea of the internet as the birth place of a 'frictionless capitalism' illustrates this repressed knowledge. We imagine that there is only a virtual economy, where the problem is to 'reduce friction' or the links between transfers of money as much as possible. Are not the internet casinos and poker sites the ultimate examples of this detachment of money from their material background – fetishism in a degree that even Karl Marx could not have imagined? The attacks on the World Trade Centre could thus be interpreted as a desperate call from the

Third World to remind us that there is still a material basis of the virtual world that we are moving around in. Just like in *The Matrix*, the computer simulated reality (the virtual economy) is a game that keeps us from confronting the harsh background of the scenery. The expression 'welcome to the desert of the real' should thus be read as an invitation to turn one's back on the old self-perception and re-interpret one's perception of reality.

One should here distinguish more precisely between Jacques Lacan's concepts of the real and reality in order to make clear the significance of the concept of the real. Reality is that which presents itself to us in the symbolic order of which we are part. It is ordered, understandable, and stable. The symbolic order is the big Other, and as we have seen, this means that it does not 'really' exist, but nonetheless functions. It gives us our reality. The real is the inherent lack within the symbolic order, it is the crack in the well ordered system, the reminder that not everything has been said or that reality is ideologically mediated by a non-existing Other. The real is in this sense a purely negative concept – the limit of the positive existence of reality. Nonetheless, the real happens. It breaks in, surprises, shocks and traumatises. The real is not something specific outside of reality, but is the fact that reality sometimes cannot contain itself, contradicts itself and is more than itself. It is the lightning that strikes, the horrifying experience, but also the revolutionary act, falling in love, and the encounter with the other (across the distances and reservations of multiculturalism!). One could say that the break-in of the real is that which makes reality real and gives the subjects a possibility to establish or relate to the order anew.

Interpreting the terror attacks of 11 September as the return of the real therefore entails seeing the event as an opportunity to reinterpret ourselves and the world. Not because we should all leave our American or American inspired suburbs and travel to Africa or Pakistan to do good, but because we must change our self-perception and realise that the post-political world is not a-political. There is, as a matter of fact, a connection between political decisions taken in the corridors of power in the Western world and the reality facing Third World countries every day. 'The U.S. just got the taste of what goes on around the world on a daily basis, from Sarajevo to Grozny, from Rwanda and Congo to Sierra Leone. If one adds to the situation in New York snipers and gang rapes, one gets an idea about what Sarajevo was a decade ago' (ibid.: 3).

The problem with our self-perception is that we imagine living in an age after politics, or refuse to see that there are political consequences from the decisions we or our representatives are making. This problem has ominous consequences for us. If network society is a reality without its own substance, then terrorism suddenly becomes the only possible form of resistance. Terrorism in other words can also be interpreted as a desperate attempt to articulate a political critique. One could see the piracy recently appearing around the Horn of Africa in a similar way. If liberalism entails a sense of having transcended actual political conflicts, i.e. if it entails the idea that there are no longer any genuine political adversaries, then people who see themselves as just that can only appear in the shape of criminals, pirates, malicious despots or terrorists.

Again, we see how liberal, Western societies receive their own message back in a perverted form. By treating oppositional groups as terrorists, one begets terrorism. The advantage in declaring war on a state is that a declaration of war is a kind of contract. One can negotiate peace with an enemy, and with a genuine political adversary one can have diplomatic connections, negotiate, etc. The 'War on Terror' is a war on an emotion or a type of act – and one cannot negotiate a peace agreement with either of these.

On the one hand, it therefore looks like that in order to take the position that was taken earlier by the (radical) political opponent, one today has to take the role of the terrorist. On the other hand, the answer to the resulting terrorism – security politics in a broad sense – can be seen as a strategy of depoliticisation characterised by a restrictive politics on certain democratic fora and assemblies and a hollowing out of some basic liberal rights. In the name of the struggle against terrorism, we must be ready to sacrifice certain liberal privileges, accept increased surveillance, restrict the right to organised opposition or even any openly expressed oppositional support, and so on. Security politics thereby comes to function as the literal reinforcement of the conviction that politics has ended and that history has found its final form – the rest is police work. This creates not only the problem of how to articulate actual and urgent political resistance around the world (could we have supported the ANC in South Africa or Solidarity in Poland on the same premises?), but also the problem of whether and how much it limits and inhibits 'our own' democratic order in the Western world. The problem becomes one of when and how we will be able to leave the vicious circle of security measures and illegal opposition, in order not to slip into some sort of permanent security based state of exception, where we, ultimately, out of consideration of 'Western values' and fundamental liberal rights, increasingly have to accept limitations and setbacks in relation to Western values and fundamental liberal rights (Žižek 2002a: 106f).

At a minimum, Žižek's alternative is that philosophical and political thinking must maintain its imaginative force and creativity to make real alternatives to this development possible. At a maximum, his demand is a kind of 'politics of the real' that installs an actual reassessment of the very foundation of society. In any case, he believes that we must give up the fantasy of the neutral, Western democracy that is innocent of power and politics, that treats all groups as equal, and which is not based on exploitation.

In the same way as the majority in a well functioning democracy must take the minority into consideration in order to create a real, balanced democratic order, the Western world in general must take the rest of the world into consideration in order to create a real, balanced world society. Žižek closes his short essay from 15 September 2001 by describing an alternative which he (still) doesn't seem too optimistic about the outcome of.

> So the alternative is: will Americans decide to fortify further their 'sphere,' or to risk stepping out of it? Either America will persist in, strengthen even the attitude of 'Why should this happen to us? Things like this don't happen HERE!', leading to more aggressivity towards the threatening Outside, in short: to a paranoiac acting out. Or, America will finally risk stepping through the fantasmatic screen separating it from the *Outside World*, accepting its arrival into the *Real World*,

making the long-overdue move from 'A thing like this should not happen HERE!' to 'A thing like this should not happen ANYWHERE!' (Žižek 2001b: 5)

In *The Matrix*, the hero faces the choice between the red and the blue pill. The blue pill will make him forget everything about the matrix, about the resistance and the encounter with the real, and give him back the innocence and bliss of ignorance – the possibility of falling asleep again. The red pill will make it possible for him to return to the real world in a new way, but will simultaneously block him from going back to the comfort and carelessness of the old world. USA picked the blue pill after 9-11, and it is still an open question whether the change in American politics after the election of President Obama in 2008 will make it possible to cough it back up again. Žižek, obviously, was for Obama in the choice between him and John McCain (indeed, he stated that it was important for the whole world that Obama would be elected – and that all citizens of the world should be allowed to vote at the election, except the Americans), but a year into his presidency it is still too early to estimate the scale of the changes that his election will effect.

Chapter 4. The revolutionary subject: Žižek's ethical and political horizon

The question concerning freedom and spontaneity has long been a problem in the Marxist tradition. How does political change come about? Through necessary laws of history – then why bother or campaign…? Perhaps through a sovereign, independent rational subject that is able to 'see what is best' and free to do as he pleases – but isn't that what bourgeois philosophers have been saying all along; you are free to choose? Žižek's move is to go back to the Cartesian *cogito*. The *cogito* in Žižek's interpretation, however, is not one that serves as the fundament of a self-conscious and self-transparent subject, but rather as the 'fundament' of a subject with a disruptive and creative power. The *cogito* can form the point of initiation of change, because it is not an existing part of the symbolic order, but rather lingers on its edge (it is represented in the symbolic by its signifier, but is not itself part of it – the signifier represents the subject for another signifier, as Lacan says).

This subject is the one that Lacan thought: the subject of the unconscious, and it marks an occasion for Žižek to reread and rethink a series of more or less repressed or forgotten positions: firstly, of course, Cartesian thinking itself; secondly Heidegger and German Idealism; and thirdly the Marxist tradition, represented by Marx, Lenin and Lukács, among others. Finally, this endeavour to step on as many toes as possible is completed by a praise of Paulinian Christianity. In all of these cases, an attempt at invoking a way of thinking revolutionary subjectivity is at the core of Žižek's reading. His Lacanian interventions are, as described in chapter 1, efforts at returning to great thinkers and making use of their critical energy in a contemporary context. Žižek writes the following about his use of Lenin – a programmatic statement that could be invoked to characterise the use he is making of most classical thinkers:

> [T]he idea is not to return to Lenin, but to *repeat* him in the Kierkegaardian sense: to retrieve the same impulse in today's constellation. The return to Lenin aims neither at nostalgically *re-enacting* the 'good old revolutionary times', nor at an opportunistic-pragmatic *adjustment* of the old programme to 'new conditions', but at *repeating*, in the present worldwide conditions, the Leninist gesture of reinventing the revolutionary project in the conditions of imperialism and colonialism ... (Žižek 2002b: 11)

Lenin rips out Marx from his original context and 'applies' him in a new one, which contributes to universalising Marx' theory. Žižek wants to do the same with Lenin – and St. Paul – and indeed with everything he meets. There is no material that is a priori immune to a critical transformation (ibid.: 267). Religion can, for instance, be 'opium to the people', but also a revolutionary force. Of course, there is a difference between whether Žižek is analysing Hollywood melodramas or Marx. In the first case, the task is to read them in ways that liberate an unknown potential from an ideological clasping or more or less explicit censorship, while in the latter the issue is much more straightforwardly one of interpreting what Marx said and 'repeating it' in the sense indicated. Common to all of Žižek's Lacanian interventions is, however, that they are searching texts, films, events and experiences for material for a renewed philosophical and conceptual activism, and not least for a radical political criticism. And the object of this criticism has a name: capitalism.

We will therefore continue our little tour around Žižek's authorship by looking more closely at the relationship between capitalism and subjectivity. Let us mention three minimally defining elements of capitalism: that our society is structured by a fundamental separation of the political from the economical; that economy has a particular status that allows it to overdetermine other, functionally differentiated societal systems; and that the most important form of social life is the form of the commodity. A critical project must take its point of departure from this diagnosis in order to indicate the potential for change.

Walter Benjamin, around 1900, saw the prostitute as the emblematic expression of capitalism – a symbol of the fact that the worker is merely a commodity – an object for sale. The prostitute, on the one hand, is the most repressed and excluded: a fallen person who is vulgar, scheming and without morals. At the same time, however, the prostitute also incarnates what we all are, namely a commodity. Like the prostitute, we are selling ourselves as commodities: as labour. This connection between the particular (the cast away, the expelled) and the universal (being an expression of a common, human condition) implies that overcoming the alienation of the prostitute is simultaneously overcoming the alienation of humankind. Benjamin's analysis is thus an update of Marx's, to whom the proletariat exactly expresses the dehumanising effects of capitalism at the same time as it carries the demand for the abolition of this societal order.

Žižek basically wants to combine this figure – the subject that is at the same time a product of a given order and capable of escaping it – with the Lacanian understanding of the subject of the unconscious. Let us therefore consider this subject more carefully in the philosophical tradition that begins with René Descartes, before we end up with the revolutionary subject. We begin with a ghost that is haunting Europe...

I think not, therefore I am

> A spectre is haunting Western academia ... the spectre of the Cartesian subject. All academic powers have entered into a holy alliance to exorcize this spectre: the New Age obscurantist (who wants to supersede the 'Cartesian paradigm' towards a new holistic approach) and the postmodern deconstructionist (for whom the Cartesian subject is a discursive fiction, an effect of decentred textual mechanisms); the Habermasian theorist of communication (who insists on a shift from Cartesian monological subjectivity to discursive intersubjectivity) and the Heideggerian proponent of the thought of Being (who stresses the need to 'traverse' the horizon of modern subjectivity culminating in current ravaging nihilism); the cognitive

> scientist (who endeavours to prove empirically that there is no unique scene of the Self, just a pandemonium of competing forces) and the Deep Ecologist (who blames Cartesian mechanicist materialism for providing the philosophical foundation for the ruthless exploitation of nature); the critical (post-) Marxist (who insists that the illusory freedom of the bourgeois thinking subject is rooted in class division) and the feminist (who emphasizes that the allegedly sexless *cogito* is in fact a male patriarchal formation). (Žižek 1999: 1)

The exorcism of the Cartesian *cogito* has been going on for quite a while. Since Roland Barthes declared the death of the author, the *cogito* has been fair game. If by the *cogito* you understand a self-conscious and monological I, then the hunt has not been in vain. But maybe this identification of the *cogito* with the worst kind of metaphysics of being is nonetheless to move too quickly. Maybe this shows a lack of will to confront the more hyperbolic aspects of the *cogito*. Often the aggressive dismissal of the *cogito* even shows more about the attempts on behalf of the aggressor to normalise the more excessive sides of the subject than it does about the *cogito* itself. In this sense, the *cogito* is still haunting us.

But what has this got to do with Marxism? The above quotation, obviously, is a paraphrase of the opening lines from the *Communist Manifesto*. Marx speaks of a ghost that haunts Europe; one that strikes terror into the Pope, the Tsar, Metternich, Guizot, French radicals and German police. These European elite, however, took their precautions and arranged a hunt for Marxism in the hope of stamping it out. But how do you kill something that has no positive existence? The *Communist Manifesto* is exactly trying to conjure up a spirit rather than to describe something tangible. Maybe Marxism is most of all a revolutionary spirit that cannot be manifested ontologically in any doctrine, and which constantly erodes distinctions between near and far, being and non-being, and the given and that which is to come. Although Marx was declared dead in many quarters after the collapse of the so-called 'really existing socialism', the exorcism in mainstream academia was never completely successful. Žižek's particular contribution could be said to consist in wanting to maintain the radicality of both the Marxist heritage and the tradition for thinking subjectivity that originally emanated from Descartes.

Žižek rebukes contemporary critics of Cartesianism for having reduced the *cogito* to nothing but a foundational being in the most conservative sense. In the critique of essentialism of the 1980s, any kind of recourse to something like a 'fundament' was seen as a conservative trait that hinders a radical democratic politics. Žižek's favourite aversions are here deconstructivism in the American cultural studies-version, Foucault – also in a cultural studies interpretation, and post-Marxism represented by Ernesto Laclau and Antonio Negri. Žižek's countermove is to claim that the ground of the subject – the *cogito* – is precisely the precondition of any revolutionary politics. There is no revolution without a revolutionary subject.

Again, we must visit Lacan and enter his reading of Descartes more carefully. Lacan's first reflection on the *cogito* can be found in the text on 'The Mirror Stage as Formative for the Function of the I', which we have touched upon earlier. In this text, Lacan claims that the psychoanalytic experience concerning the formation of the I had the inevitable conclusion that any philosophy based on the *cogito* had to be criticised, meaning any philosophy that takes as its point of departure a self-conscious and monological I. Lacan thus immediately seems to have joined the hunting down of the *cogito* that Žižek is making a parody of. This, however, is not at all the case.

The child 'experiences' its own 'completeness' when it looks into a mirror. Here it sees an autonomous and self-carrying individual – an experience which often causes great joy in the child. The mirror, as already stated, is not necessarily to be understood literally, since the child can also reflect itself in the care of its surroundings (often of the mother) or even more generally simply in the surroundings (the social). What the child recognises in the reflection is its 'I'. The central point of Lacanian psychoanalysis, and that which separates it from ego-psychology, is now that the 'I' or the ego is not the same as the subject. The subject, namely, is the remainder that is produced in the identification of the I, or: the subject is the split between the subject in a 'public I' – the one that looks just like me – and the unconscious. The subject of psychoanalysis is that which was not reflected in the mirroring, or is the fact that the symbolic and imaginary identities of the subject are always established on the background of a lack.

Descartes' mistake was that he did not draw sufficient conclusions from the difference between these levels of the subject. It was, truly, the ability to think and doubt that drew René Descartes from his comfortable armchair to the only thing that could not be doubted: *that* doubt or thinking is going on, i.e. to the *cogito*. But from this realisation that something is thought, he wrongfully concluded that that which thinks must be the same as that which was sitting in the armchair before the occurrence of doubt. 'I think, therefore I am – the same as before'. Lacan refuses to recognise the validity of this sentence. Thinking consists in questioning identity, not in legitimising it. When the questioning, which doubt initiates, has been carried through, there is only the pure position of enunciation left: I think, therefore I am *not* a Frenchman sitting in an armchair. There is no innocent way back to the mirror image or the identification with the being I. As Mladen Dolar has put it:

> One can start with a simple observation about Descartes' own procedure in the *Meditations*, the procedure of a 'methodical doubt,' which can be seen as a gradual reduction of consciousness, its 'evacuation.' Consciousness must lose any worldly support, it must be cleansed of any objective counterpart. ... What eventually remains, is a pure vanishing point without a counterpart, which can only be sustained in a minimal gesture of enunciation. ... Descartes himself considered alternative suggestions of 'I doubt, I err, I lie,' etcetera, *ergo sum*, the minimal form of which is 'I enounce, *ergo sum*.' ... What remains is purely an empty spot occupied by the subject of enunciation. (Dolar 1998: 15)

Lacan, and Lacanians like Dolar and Žižek, differentiate between the subject of thinking, enunciation, and the subject of being, the enunciated. The subject of the enunciated is the being (*ergo sum*) that is expressed in the sentence. The enunciation is the position of the subject when it enunciates or thinks (*cogito*). These two never coincide entirely. The Cartesian *thinking* subject is now the subject of the unconscious in as far as it is the secret distance to the *being* subject of the enunciated. Thinking is going on, where I am not. Or: I am, in as far as I do not think. Our ordinary, everyday I and its doings are in this particular sense 'thoughtless' – in most of what we do, we are not aware of what and why we are doing it. But in acting and reacting, we are nonetheless taking certain, specific positions that we might not be conscious of. The position of enunciation is therefore the position of thinking – it goes on, while we *are*. Whether we know it or not, thinking is going on, on our behalf, if you will.

A nice example to illustrate these different paraphrases of the relation between the subjects of thinking and being has been provided by a students' magazine (*Doxa*) at the University of Aarhus in Denmark. The students cut out a commercial slogan from a well known kitchen hardware supplier and placed it under a picture of poor, starving people in a refugee camp. The slogan said: 'Everyone is entitled to a great kitchen!' The enunciated of this expression remained the same, thoughtless motto. But by manipulating the position from which it was enunciated, the magazine managed to create a thoughtful interpretation of the position that a commercial statement, claiming that a great kitchen is something like a human right, takes in a broader context. It is thinking more than it knows.

Think of Lacan's *dictum* (analysed in chapter 2) that a madman who believes that he is a king is no more crazy than a king who believes that he is a king. A king, who believes that he is a king, identifies completely and unproblematically with his symbolic mandate and thereby forgets the difference between the subject of the enunciated and the subject of the enunciation – he doesn't *think*. Therefore he is as mad, or thoughtless, as the madman. One could say that the king's interpretation of Descartes' *dictum* is: 'I think not, therefore I am (a king)'. Is not this exactly what is wrong with powerful leaders that remain in power too long? They stop thinking and identify with their reflection entirely. This is of course what is at the core of the expression that power corrupts: the longer one upholds it, the more convinced one is likely to be that it is one's 'natural' position.

So, let us once again return to the mirror image. What I see is what

I am. But what I do *not* see is the medium of thinking: 'Why am I like this?' (and not in another way). This distance is what makes possible a disruption or emancipation from the symbolic mandate of the subject, and it therefore also relates to the problem of multiculturalism described earlier. The real recognition of another human being would not be to recognise him or her as a representative from a culture or an ethnicity, but to recognise his or her subjectivity as the ability to 'see oneself from the outside', or to maintain, for example, a critical or ironic distance to one's own identity. Therefore, ironically, there is more potential for 'cross-cultural encounters' in insults, misunderstandings, slips, etc. than in multicultural recognition: only in such situations is a universal space opened up for the encounter. I think (enunciate), therefore I am (not my symbolic mandate). One could say that in order to meet and respect one another as thinking beings, we must be open towards each other as *more* than the public identities and roles that we perform in virtue of culture, religion, work, etc.

But back to the *cogito*. It is important for Lacan to emphasise that the *cogito* remains empty. The distance to the symbolic and imaginary does not point back to a real core or substance that could be reached in meditation – not even in Cartesian meditations. The unconscious remains unconscious. The *cogito* cannot, like Descartes attempted, be transformed into a *res cogitans* (a thinking thing). The Cartesian *cogito* is therefore the subject of the unconscious, because it appears as the very distance to the subject that is.

> Cogito marks a 'non-place,' a gap, a chasm in the chain of being, it doesn't delineate a certain sphere of being to be placed alongside other spheres, it cannot be situated in some part of reality, yet it is at the same time correlative to reality as such. (ibid.: 16)

Lacan's references to Descartes were ill received in his time, and this was not ameliorated by the fact that he also claimed that Descartes' references to God were radically modern. Lacan's point was that in order to 'get back into the world' from the exile of the *cogito* after the radical doubt, Descartes had to rely on an authority that could guarantee the stability of the symbolic order. Effectively, the end of the line in radical doubt could only be reconnected with the chain of being via an ultimate guarantor that could not possibly want to deceive the subject. The subject had to rely on a master signifier. One signifier had to be pulled out from the referential structure of language in order to be able to form a transcendental centre for all references. Such a position could be attributed to God, the nation or the people. The fact that Descartes' radical doubt led him towards the divine was no surprise to Lacan. Simultaneously, however, he claimed that the reference to the divine was an attempt at denying or repressing the lack. The imagination of a master is a necessary and productive illusion, but it is still an illusion. Without a master, no *ergo sum* (Žižek 2000a: 72). Or in other words: in order to have a conception of the world or a place in the world at all, the subject must rely on a fundamental fantasmatic structure. In terms of the critique of ideology, this precisely means that there is no objective, neutral place outside of ideology.

One could, as Lacan, claim that the choice is between being and thinking. But in a sense, the choice has already been made. It has the same structure as the proverbial choice between 'your money or your life': the money is not worth anything, if you don't have your life. The subject must choose life; it must alienate itself in the symbolic order – in language and the social. 'Thinking' must be given up in favour of being, but thinking nonetheless carries on in the guise of the unconscious. Lacan paraphrases and interprets Descartes' motto in a multitude of ways, as we have already suggested. Other versions than those already mentioned are: 'I think where I am not, therefore I am where I do not think'; 'I am not wherever I am the plaything of my thought'; 'I think of what I am where I do not think to think' (Lacan 1977: 166). The central point being that one cannot infer directly from thinking (qua the unconscious) to being (qua the symbolic), from *cogito* to sum. Almost as a programmatic statement, one could say that for Žižek it precisely becomes the task of philosophy to articulate thinking in the midst of being, not least via the many inversions and surprising questions.

Let us move towards Žižek's use of this insight: his way of bringing forward the 'ghost' that haunts Western academia, and which must be transformed into the political, revolutionary, struggling subject. We will begin like *The Ticklish Subject* with Žižek's discussion of Heidegger's interpretation of the transcendental imagination. In Žižek's reading of Heidegger, as in many other places, it is the relation between thinking and being which is central. Roughly said, the move is to claim that it was Heidegger's subordination of 'thinking' (the unconscious, the *cogito*) under being (qua being-thrown (*Geworfenheit*), being-in-the-world), which in fact weakened his power of resistance against Nazi propaganda. The other side of the argument is therefore a defence of the madness of the cogito: of its unruliness, of freedom, spontaneity, and revolution.

The Proletarian

In the first essay of *The Ticklish Subject*, Heidegger's relation to Nazism is discussed. This was one of the most enigmatic scandals of philosophy in the twentieth century: one of its greatest thinkers, Martin Heidegger, was a member of the Nazi party in the 1930s. Often, this biographical circumstance is explained by Heidegger's peculiar and somewhat naïve personality or by coincidences that have nothing do to with his work, or the entire affair is dismissed (he was not a member for that long and was later critical of the form that Nazism actually took in Germany, etc.). In the past couple of decades, however, some researchers have tried to establish the connection between Heidegger the person and the philosopher in order to investigate and emphasise the danger of a certain kind of thinking of being that was prominently displayed in Heidegger's main work, *Sein und Zeit* from 1927. These attempts do not always have very elegant results – often so much politics is read into Heidegger's thinking of being that they effectively find what they themselves have installed.

Žižek's attempt is in this context a moderate one and relatively loyal to Heidegger (who was in fact also one of Žižek's first philosophical heroes). Nonetheless, he too tries to locate the background or an explanation of Heidegger's political mistake in his philosophy. The argument is that it was Heidegger's reluctance to think the madness of the subject which made him vulnerable to Nazi propaganda.

The exploration and emphasis of the 'thrownness' of *Dasein* and its fundamental being-in-the-world led Heidegger in the direction of an existential communitarianism, which ultimately offered a way for the subject to be dissolved in the ritualised mass movement of Nazism. Thereby, a betrayal of the freedom and spontaneity of the subject is also indicated. Žižek believes this problematic to be especially clear in Heidegger's reading of Kant's writings on transcendental imagination.

Žižek opens the discussion of Heidegger by pointing out that his point of departure is a productive one. Heidegger's ontology is political. Heidegger's *Dasein* is 'thrown', but it is simultaneously 'throwing' (itself), and there is nothing 'outside' or 'underneath' this situation that can provide objective criteria for how the circle of 'throwing' and 'being thrown' should be lived or exercised. Politics, similarly, is exactly characterised by decisions being made without the presence of an ultimate ontological fundament. Žižek therefore rebukes Habermas' critique of Heidegger for irrational decisionism and an accompanying refusal of any kind of universal normative criterion of political activity.

> [W]hat this criticism rejects as proto-Facist decisionism is simply the basic condition of the *political*. In a perverted way, Heidegger's Nazi engagement was therefore a 'step in the right direction', a step towards openly admitting and fully assuming the consequences of the lack of ontological guarantee, of the abyss of human freedom. (Žižek 1999: 20f).

Heidegger's fundamental mistake, however, was that he gave up the idea of transcendental subjectivity. A certain fear of the Cartesian spectre can be found in the structure of *Dasein*, Being-There, and its being-in-the-world. Our existential projects are always exercised on the background of an already existing and impenetrable (life)world. Against Heidegger, Žižek claims that an unconscious must be added to this life-world in order to make a radical break with it possible. 'The "Unconscious" is the crack that makes the subject's primordial stance something other than "being-in-the-world"' (ibid.: 62).

Žižek claims that Heidegger's reading of Kant's theory of transcendental imagination is influenced by the same attempt at downplaying the hyperbolic sides of subjectivity. This reading, to be fair, is not without corroboration in Kant's own texts. Like Heidegger, Kant also seems to have wanted to normalise and neutralise the excessive aspects of the subject. In an attempt to break free from this reading, Žižek points out that transcendental imagination has a 'negative side' as well. Its function is not only to create a synthesis of the manifold in sensual impression, like Kant seemed to believe. It also separates that which immediately appears as a unity (ibid.: 32). Like a sensual impression that must be synthesised into a unity in order to become a meaningful experience (say, when a bunch of colours and sounds become the experience of a brook), the experiencing subject must also tear apart the unity it is part of, in order to be able to focus on a limited and meaningful experience – a *specific* manifold for the synthesis (the *brook* and not the bank, the animals, the air, the rain or everything else around). Kant focused on the synthesis, Žižek focuses on the rupture.

There is a name for this disruptive force in psychoanalysis: death drive. The death drive constantly derails the subject in its efforts at establishing fullness of being, and the death drive is therefore in contrast to the fantasm, which for Lacan is precisely the product of the subject's attempt at synthesising the manifold, the hybrid, and the fragmentary. The fantasm is 'freezing' desire and thereby the subject in rigid patterns of behaviour. Death drive is the name of the opposite movement – of the derailment of the subject's symbolically mediated acts of identification.

> My contention is that the Freudian death drive, which has nothing whatsoever to do with some 'instinct' that pushes us towards (self-)destruction, is precisely his name for this 'transformation of the being of man in the sense of a *derangement* of his position among beings'. (Žižek 2000b: 82)

One could therefore be tempted to translate the 'positive' and 'negative' sides of transcendental imagination into fantasmatic desire and death drive, respectively. The subject is essentially 'given' in the struggle between these two forces. Desire leads the subject in the direction of ideologies, which offer ways of covering its lack, while death drive leads the subject away from these, or makes it possible for the subject to resist and fight ideologies.

The hyperbolic subjectivity, which Heidegger neglected, is the precondition of revolutionary practice. The revolutionary event becomes possible when people risk their freedom and give up on the usual calculations of winning and losing, and for a moment cancel the causality of the symbolic. 'Death' in death drive therefore does not signal the end of earthly life, but much rather a new beginning (ibid.).

Much Marxism has been stuck in the idea that any revolutionary change has to take the working class as its point of departure. The 'ideal' has been dirty, hard working industrial workers. It has been discussed whether small, private farmers were poor enough; whether one could be progressive, if one had changed from overalls to a suit. The central point for Žižek, however, is not the particular attributes of a certain group, but its placement in relation to the whole of capitalism. The proletariat for Marx is the symbol of a universal humanity – and as such it points towards a society beyond exploitation and humiliation. For Žižek, the important point is not whether the proletariat was or is the most suppressed class, but whether its existence embodies the internal contradictions and imbalances of capitalism.

One must therefore distinguish between the working class as a social group (as placed within the social matrix, as majority) and the proletariat as an agent, which in a militant way struggles for 'universal truth' (as the group that breaks with the social matrix, as minority) (Žižek 1999: 226f). There is no necessary connection between these two groups. The crucial point is therefore whether one is answering to the idea of a system beyond the exploitation and impoverishment of capitalism, or whether one is fighting for one's own privileges. Should the struggle be understood as a struggle for positions within the same social matrix, or is the struggle a struggle for a new and radically different society?

Class struggle is not initially a struggle between classes, but rather a struggle to cover up or make apparent the flaws and inconsistencies of capitalism. The danger of perceiving class struggle as the struggle for recognition and rights, for example, is that it thereby supports fixed identities and social roles – and in effect capitalism as a system. Class struggle and classes themselves are not that which all social phenomena can be reduced to, but rather a generative matrix that conditions the different ideological horizons, through which society is attributed meaning (Žižek 2002b: 190).

> [A] class society in which the ideological perception of the class division was pure and direct would be a harmonious structure with no struggle – or to put it in Laclau's terms, class antagonism would thereby be fully symbolized; it would no longer be impossible/real, but a simple differential structural feature. (Žižek 1999: 187)

Žižek's view of the proletariat is strongly inspired by Hegel's thoughts of the *Lumpenproletariat*. This group was exactly characterised by not being contemplated as a class *sui generis*. For Žižek, similarly, the proletariat is the group that does not fit into the capitalist whole. Revolutionary struggle is therefore not a struggle for more salary, for instance, as such a struggle will only make certain displacements within a given system possible. Any political act that is taking its point of departure in particular identities and their demands – whether they be ethnic, religious, sexual or simply different lifestyles – remains reactionary (Žižek 2003: 132f). Revolutionary struggle, on the contrary, questions the symbolic itself – the fact that the being of the worker is reduced to a commodity.

Žižek here makes a move similar to Jacques Rancière, who links the revolutionary with the political. Politics, for both, emerged in ancient Greece when some members of the *demos* not only demanded to be heard and compensated for their sufferings, but also started speaking on behalf of society. They criticised those in power for suiting their own interests and not serving the good of society. Politics as such is therefore the short circuit of the universal (speaking on behalf of humanity) and the particular (doing it as someone excluded): a paradoxical universal singularity, which steps into the empty place of the universal and destabilises the social whole (ibid.: 65). In this sense, politics is in sharp contrast to the post-political complaining subjectivity of identity politics. When, for instance, the dispossessed or women have been included into the democratic order, it has not only increased the number of those who participate in the democratic process, but more radically changed what one can understand by democracy at all.

A third concept could be linked to the chain of revolution and politics, namely freedom. Freedom is precisely the ability to transcend the coordinates of a given situation and establish the conditions for the situation in which one is acting. The actions that are performed on the background of the explicit or implicit rules of a given social matrix are in this perspective unfree, while the break with the matrix itself is free, since it generates a new scheme of interpretation (Žižek 2001c: 115, 122). Revolutionary politics is therefore not nihilist. The central part of a revolution, and that which separates it from mere destruction, is the transformation of revolutionary energy into a new social order. It is only once this has been established that one can say that an event has been revolutionary – a revolution is only revolutionary when it is recognised as such, i.e. if it succeeds. The hard work is waiting the day after the revolutionary explosion. How can one remain faithful to the revolution (Žižek 2003: 135)?

A big debate within Marxism has been about when the time is ripe for revolution, and by 'ripe' it is partly meant the conscious awareness of the working class, and partly the development of the means of production. Žižek here takes Lenin's side against those who argue for reformist advances. The time for revolution never becomes ripe, if we accept the basic premises of reformism, or better: the revolution is restructuring the system on the background of which it is possible to perceive the moment as ripe or unripe. In other words: one must 'plunge ahead' into an apparently unripe situation and change its coordinates so that it will, *post hoc*, appear to have been ripe after all (Žižek 2001a: 114). It therefore makes no sense to talk about an objective logic, which history or more specifically the control of the means of production should follow. Those who wait for the time to be ripe will be bound to the prevailing logic (ibid.: 133). History might on the surface seem to be following iron laws, not the least because the events and stages of the past are always interpreted in light of the present. The non-realised and wasted opportunities, the contingency of history, are therefore only revealed with great difficulty or not at all.

In consequence of this, one can also say that it is not the case that certain specific demands – sexual emancipation, less working hours, co-ownership, etc. – are by nature always revolutionary: particular demands may have revolutionary potential at a certain moment and shortly after be accommodated easily. A good example is monogamy. It was seen by many as essential to the reproduction of the labour force, and some therefore thought that 'perverted' practises had emancipatory potential (flower power, S/M, free sex, etc.). Today, there is almost no sexual practice which is not accommodated within the confines of capitalism. The conclusion to be made from this, however, is not...

> that capitalism has the endless ability to integrate, and thus cut off, the subversive edge of all particular demands – the question of timing, of 'seizing the moment', is crucial here. A certain particular demand possesses, at a certain moment, a global detonating power; it functions as a metaphorical stand-in for the global revolution: if we insist on it unconditionally, the system will explode; if, however, we wait too long, the metaphorical short circuit between this particular demand and global overthrow is dissolved, and the System can, with sneering hypocritical satisfaction, make the gesture of 'You wanted this? Now you've got it!', without anything really radical happening. (ibid.: 116f)

How then, to decide whether something is genuinely revolutionary? The simple and rather imprecise answer must be: when the social order has been radically changed; when nothing is the same any more. After Schoenberg, composers cannot compose romantic works anymore, after Kandinsky and Picasso, one cannot paint figuratively anymore, and after Joyce and Kafka, one cannot write realistically anymore. Or at least: all these classical styles and forms have lost their innocence, and works that follow them will, after the mentioned breaks, appear as nostalgic imitations (Žižek 2002b: lxxxvi). Was the introduction of socialism then, in this context, a revolution? Yes, it was. Even though the revolution failed in numerous ways – it did not bring freedom, but new forms of coercion – it did open a horizon of comparison to which it could be said to have failed miserably (ibid.: 131). Conversely, Nazism was not a genuine revolution, precisely because it left the social matrix intact. There was capitalism before, during and after Nazism (Žižek 1999: 140). The identification of the character of a given social matrix is therefore crucial. And this, naturally, brings us to the identification of what for Žižek today is the most crucial feature of society – namely that we are still existing within the framework of a capitalist formation of society.

It is the *economy*, stupid!

Žižek's point of departure is that the economy is not just one among different social spheres. Economy has a 'proto-transcendental' status, which means that it is a 'generative matrix' of phenomena that immediately seem to have nothing to do with economy. One could talk, for instance, about the commodification of culture and politics. Economy as the shape or form of culture has gained universal signification (Daly/Žižek 2004: 147). Let us briefly try to describe this form.

One serious flaw in many earlier analyses of capitalism has been to overlook that capitalism itself has a fundamental, almost revolutionary drive. Capitalism lives from change. Change of what? Of anything but the fundamental condition that the formation of society remains capitalist. Capitalism is an immanent system that keeps expanding its borders. This expansion should not be explained by factors outside of capitalism itself – hence its immanence. In fact, we only have to read Marx, who wrote that everything stable and solid evaporates and everything holy is undressed (Marx/Engels 1998). Think about fashion. It is precisely given by a rapid and endless metamorphosis, where new fashion always reduces the former to something unfashionable.

What is lying behind this process? On the one hand, of course, the expansion of capitalism itself. Profit is sought. Money is supposed to generate more money – it is as simple as that. The precondition of this, on the other hand, is a continued stimulation of demand. In capitalism, one does not produce merely to fulfil already given needs. It is just as important, and at least as defining, to produce needs which the

94 The Subject of Politics

consumer did not know that he or she had to begin with. Advertising is not just about informing the consumer that the DVD-player costs £10 less in one supermarket than in another, but also about convincing the client that they need a DVD-player at all.

Capital seeks ever new territories. Every time a new 'narration' appears, new options for capitalisation open up. So, perhaps gays and lesbians do not reproduce a classical patriarchal structure. No problem! You can always produce clothing, magazines, open bars, shops, and other stuff with a particular focus on this target group. In other words, capitalism is doing fine without a homogenising superstructure. It needs no truth and no history with a capital H. Capitalism lives from the particular and the multitude in the myriads of culturally defined sub groupings. What we buy in the market is not so much material objects as it is experiences and identity:

> Michel Foucault's notion of turning one's Self itself into a work of art thus finds unexpected confirmation: I buy my bodily fitness by visiting fitness clubs; I buy my spiritual enlightenment by enrolling in transcendental meditation courses; I buy my public persona by going to restaurants frequented by people with whom I want to be associated. (Žižek 2002b: 287)

For many, this multitude is the source of new liberties as an opportunity to create oneself; finally the yoke of uniformity has been lifted from our shoulders. One could of course focus on the rapid change, but it is easy to forget that behind this production of difference lies the logic of capital. We can realise ourselves as much as we like, as long as we do not question the most fundamental order (Žižek 2001a: 122). The freedom to realise oneself is therefore a very restricted kind of freedom. It is the freedom to choose between Jay Leno and David Letterman or between Coke and Pepsi.

Paradoxically, that which is excluded in late capitalist society, where we have the right to choose everything, is choice itself, the authentic choice. The choices we can make are mostly choices between commodities that perform the same or no function at all. Already as little children we have to choose between several different flavours of the same jam, three kinds of cheese, etc. just to get something to eat for breakfast. We are fed with the impression that we are constantly making important, identity forming choices, while at the same time we are really positing our freedom in the endless manifold of commodities that capitalism offers. Life becomes a multiple choice adventure, where we move around in a story with fixed frames and limits and a storyline constructed from an overwhelming amount of little concrete choices, in order to create the illusion that it is a story we are narrating ourselves.

It is of essence to connect this diagnosis of freedom and the conditions of choice with an analysis of the functioning of late capitalism. The flipside of the freedom to choose between jobs, for instance, is the lack of security in jobs, and the responsibility for making 'wrong choices' becomes individualised. When you are out of work, it is because you have chosen the wrong courses, have not optimised your CV, etc. Choices are seen as the expression of one's personal profile and not as something that has its background in one's being pushed and hassled around by market forces (Žižek 2001b: 116).

Furthermore, the much talk about self-creation and self-realisation should not make us blind to the fact that classical manual labour is still being performed on large scale in the Third World. One merely has to look at the inscription in most mass produced consumption products. 'Made in... (China, Indonesia, Bangladesh, Guatemala)' (Žižek 2001a: 134). The distinction between capital and labour is not necessarily to be made within a single nation, but is today much rather to be made between first and third world countries. One could and should of course distinguish between those that are made entirely superfluous by capitalist world economy (many of the inhabitants of poor countries who are not even 'worth' exploiting), those who work hard in the unhealthy sweatshops of 'second' and 'third' world countries, and then workers in the West, Japan and a number of new economies, who might be much better off, but are still subjected to the imperatives of capital.

Postmodernism as the new ideological superstructure of capitalism

If we focus on Western societies for a moment again, which superstructure fits late modern capitalism best? The answer must be postmodern identity politics. The politics of identity has as a central feature exactly the repression of the class perspective, which in turn implies that the endless amounts of particular identity struggles remain busy solving problems. They fight to reduce suffering, but the background of it cannot be addressed adequately within the political frame of identity politics. We can therefore place identity politics and multiculturalism in a broader, political context:

> So we are fighting our PC battles for the right of ethnic minorities, of gays and lesbians, of different lifestyles, and so forth, while capitalism pursues its triumphant march – and today's critical theory, in the guise of 'cultural studies', is performing the ultimate service for the unrestrained development of capitalism by actively participating in the ideological effort to render its massive presence invisible: in the predominant form of postmodern 'cultural criticism', the very mention of capitalism as a world system tends to give rise to accusations of 'essentialism', 'fundamentalism', and so on. The price of this depoliticization of the economy is that the domain of politics itself is in a way depoliticized: political struggle proper is transformed into the cultural struggle for the recognition of marginal identities and the tolerance of differences. (Žižek 1999: 218)

The class and commodity structure of capitalism is overdetermining society as a whole, and it is this overdetermination which identity politics is repressing. 'Class antagonism certainly appears as one in the series of social antagonisms, but it is simultaneously the specific antagonism which predominates over the rest, whose relations thus assign rank and influence to the others. It is a general illumination which bathes all the other colours and modifies their particularity.' (Žižek 2000c: 320). Identity politics reduces the question concerning economy to one among several questions on an equal level. Two fatal consequences follow from this. Firstly, the narratives about a transformation from an essentialist Marxism to a postmodern Marxism hide the fact that this break with essentialism relates to an actual historical process. The multitude and non-essentialist manifold which is celebrated by the new left is something which has fundamentally only become possible through capital's constant transgression of its own limits.

Secondly, and related to the former point, the focus on particular struggles means that one gives up any serious attempt at transgressing capitalism. When Laclau and others with him give the reader a choice between class struggle (Marxism) or postmodernity (identity politics), then the problem is not only that they make the wrong choice (i.e. deny Marxism), but also, and more fundamentally, that they do not see that capital itself has become postmodern. And further, that there is a speculative connection between capitalism and postmodern identity politics. The latter serves postmodern capitalism as its perfect superstructure.

> The passage from 'essentialist' Marxism to postmodern contingent politics (in Laclau), or the passage from sexual essentialism to contingent gender-formation (in Butler), or – a further example – the passage from metaphysician to ironist in Richard Rorty, is not a simple epistemological progress but part of the global change in the very nature of capitalist society. (Žižek 2000a: 106)

The central question after this conclusion becomes one over the kind of politics that makes possible a break with capitalism, and this is where Žižek turns to Marxism for a way to think revolutionary change. We earlier defined the political as the process in which particular demands are elevated from being an expression of particular interests to being demands of a universal restructuring of the societal order. Postmodern identity politics on this background appears to be fundamentally apolitical. It is exactly characterised by the caretaking of particular interests, and this is not fundamentally changed by forming rainbow coalitions or the like. What these 'policies' basically do,

98 The Subject of Politics

and this is what makes them reactionary, is to reinforce already existing social positions (Žižek 1999: 208). The lack of a focus on economy in postmodern identity politics means that it is simply not political enough. The critique against economic essentialism turns into a prohibition on making the function of economy a theme at all, which in turn means that the new left, exemplified by Laclau, Butler, and Rorty, are not capable of distinguishing between the contingency that is made possible within a given order and the exclusions on which this order rests (Žižek 2000a: 108).

The right to narrate, which is the point of departure of identity politics, is blocking the universalisation of specific demands. We have already discussed that. But there are other problems as well. Identity politics is morally blind. Yes, all 'progressives' support the rights of gays and lesbians. But what about the right of bikers to their lifestyle – driving Harleys really fast, being tattooed and controlling drug sales. Should young guests in night clubs have a right to take drugs – this is a kind of lifestyle as well, isn't it? Do parents have a right to circumcise their daughters if it is part of their tradition to do so? Or should the Nazis have a right to march through town, spread propaganda and recruit young supporters? Identity politics seems to be able to legitimise anything, which is why Žižek opts for Lenin and the right to *truth* rather than the right to narrate (Žižek 2002b: 177). Capital treats life forms as a colonial master treats the natives: they are studied carefully and respected. Moral involvement is never at stake – one could rather speak of indifference.

Another problem is that there is no limit to the particularisation of demands and thereby the division of groups that need special treatment: lesbians, Afro-American lesbians, Afro-American lesbian mothers, Afro-American lesbian single mothers... Where does this sub-division end? 'Postmodernists' do not seem to have an answer for that. Žižek does. It stops precisely where the particular demands can no longer be universalised. The issue is not how specific a group and its demands are, but whether these may serve as a radical criticism of a given formation or not (Žižek 1999: 203–204). What also seems to be forgotten is that anti-essentialism and relativism make for a position of strength, i.e. a position that can only be taken from a privileged, distanced position of supervision. It is the position from which all substantial positioning can be dismissed as essentialism, fundamentalism, primitivism, dogmatism or similar 'isms'. The anti-essentialist position is imagined to be an unprejudiced, neutral position. But this 'neutrality' is fake. It is a kind of 'universalism' which in reality supports only one given and particular societal order – capitalism (Žižek 2001d: 103). The reference to objectively given economic limitations or 'Development' as it is called today seems to be the card that trumps everything. If it is played, there seems to be no way around adjusting and renouncing. Žižek's strategy is to change the rules of the game so that such trumps lose their significance.

St. Paul on the barricade

We have now gone through the question of revolutionary and reactionary consciousness within a philosophical and political context, respectively. A third context is the religious. One of Žižek's observations is that, paradoxically enough, the religious superstructure that serves capitalism best is Eastern and not a Western inspired spirituality. If Max Weber had been alive, he might have written a supplementary volume to his famous work on the connection between production forms and religious orientation, entitled 'Taoist ethics and the spirit of capitalism' (Žižek 2001c: 15). The perfect superstructure of capitalism is a Western Buddhism or a New Age Gnosticism with an imperative of letting oneself go with the stream.

> 'Western Buddhism' ... enables you to fully participate in the frantic pace of the capitalist game while sustaining the perception that you are not really in it, that you are well aware how worthless this spectacle is – what really matters to you is the peace of the inner Self to which you know you can always withdraw... (ibid.: 15)

For Žižek this basically means religion without religion: a religion characterised by a cynical distance – a religion which is little more than a lifestyle and where the ethical engagement is not accompanied by a personal price to pay. If Žižek has to express admiration for a religious personality, it is (as mentioned in chapter 2) the Pope (*in casu* John Paul II) who stubbornly insists that there is a price to pay if ethics is to be genuine (ibid.: 181). But is religion an entirely reactionary force, which like opium for the people makes it susceptible to the demands of capital? No, religion may also function as a revolutionary force. The central question then becomes: which kind of religion? Žižek's answer, quoting Chesterton, is not without some provocative force: Christian orthodoxy. 'People have fallen into a foolish habit of speaking of orthodoxy as something heavy, humdrum, and safe. There never was anything so perilous or so exciting as orthodoxy' (Chesterton in Žižek 2003: 35). Furthermore, there is a natural alliance between Christianity and Marxism. Both are revolutionary ideologies that address suppression – in the shape of 'excremental identification': in Marxism with the proletarian; in Christianity with the expelled, the demeaned and the poor. Jesus was a revolutionary, and Christianity is in fact about transgressing the legalist logic of 'an eye for an eye'. Instead of an eye for an eye, we receive the demand to turn the other cheek (which makes it possible to break with the old tradition of revenge and establish an entirely new standard of justice) (Žižek 2001c: 49).

Christ himself incarnates a singular universality: on the one side, he is a cast away, excluded being, and on the other the sublime incarnation of humanity (and of the divine). Christ is thereby inscribed into the social field in the same way as the proletarian. He is included and excluded at the same time, or with Agamben we could say that he is included *as* excluded. As we have seen, it is this 'excremental' position that gives Christ the opportunity to announce the coming of a new system. Or better: Christ does not pay our debts. He does not restore a cosmic balance, but gives us the opportunity of acting freely and responsibly. When one repeats the gesture of Christ, one chooses life rather than merely living it (ibid.: 105).

The universality that Christ incarnates is not just a 'neutral container', but a 'struggling universality' (Žižek 2003: 199). To determine this activist aspect, Žižek draws on the Paulinian conception of love: *agape*. *Agape* is, in Žižek's interpretation, the force that demands from us that we break away from the organic community that we have been born into or are situated in. *Agape* is described as a kind of state of exception that suspends one's normal emotional condition (ibid.: 112–113). Žižek's examples are radical: Medea, who kills her own children; Abraham, who makes himself ready to sacrifice his only son; or God, who gives up his son. Or finally, and perhaps even more provocatively: Judas. Judas sacrifices himself in order to make it possible that the prophecy of the Messiah will come true: an act which has the price, apart from losing his master and friend, of eternal condemnation (ibid.: 16–17).

Agape is not the principle of loving one's neighbour – at least not if the commandment of charity is understood in the usual sense. You must love your neighbour, because your neighbour is, at the end of the day, a good person or the same as you. Žižek rarely refers to this commandment (he is not trying to articulate some sort of secular Christian humanism), but more frequently to Jesus' scandalous demand that one must hate one's father and mother and even oneself (Žižek 2000b: 120). Hate is not the opposite of *agape*; hate *is agape* – the demand of breaking out from 'original', organic communities. It is a hatred of the existing social matrix and the subject positions that it sustains. *Agape* is 'love itself that enjoins us to 'unplug' from the organic community into which we were born. ... Christianity asserts as the highest act precisely what pagan wisdom condemns as the source of Evil: the gesture of *separation*, of drawing the line, of clinging to an element that disturbs the balance of all' (ibid.: 121). The work of St. Paul, for Žižek, implies dissociation from any kind of communitarianism. His goal is not only to unite different groups with their agenda and needs, but to create a collective that struggles for an unconditional universalism.

Hating the other thus means hating his inscription into the social matrix. It does not mean that behind this inscription lies an untouched, uncorrupted self, but precisely that we, out of love for the other, must overturn the system that is demeaning him. *Agape* is not about mercy (like giving charity and thereby redeeming one's bad conscience), but about indignation, which thereby leads to revolutionary change.

Žižek's Christianity is an activist, political doctrine. One might want to call it fundamentalist, which Žižek himself has accepted as praise on some occasions. A number of figures from his Marxism do appear to have common traits with the Christian tradition: the 'excremental identification', the struggling universality and the demand for political organisation, which transforms the struggling to more than a numeric multitude. What is still missing, in a way, is only the idea of a revolutionary moment: those magic moments when the religious energy manifests itself. The parallel in Christian discourse is the imagination of the absolute.

> [W]hat *is* the Absolute? Something that appears to us in fleeting experiences – say, through the gentle smile of a beautiful woman, or even through the warm, caring smile of a person who may otherwise seem ugly and rude: in such miraculous but *extremely fragile* moments, another dimension transpires through our reality. As such, the Absolute is easily corroded; it slips all too easily through our fingers and must be handled as carefully as a butterfly. (ibid.: 128)

With the absolute, we are confronted with the radical break once again. The absolute breaks our usual rhythm. The beauty of a woman passing by suddenly makes us stop. The smile breaks off an otherwise aggressive dialogue. These essentially revolutionary moments can be 'caught in the air' and have enormous importance. Or they can be denied or isolated and everything will remain the same. Precisely in the same way as the right moment for revolutionary changes can be missed.

Communism, of course!

Žižek praises revolution in ways that can sometimes seem a bit obsessive, but he is not utopian in the usual sense of the word. In fact, his work is devoid of any positive version of a societal structure that would be better than capitalism and liberal democracy. One can choose to see this as a weakness or a strength. Žižek believes that what immediately seems like superficial crises and problems are really structural problems – much like Marx himself thought. These crises do not make the system explode by itself – we are not talking some kind of vulgar evolutionism – but change can be articulated from within the system itself. Žižek's criticism is thus an immanent criticism, and some would argue that the changes he is hoping and cheering for would gain a bit more momentum if he could offer some indication of what a future society might look like, as if 'from outside' our current situation.

That being said, one could also turn the problematic around. Critique does not necessarily become less urgent because of the absence of an explicit, alternative vision. Injustice and indignity are phenomena that are reflected back onto the system that produces them, and the social indignation does contain, in the negative, if you will, a vision of another future society. The combination of the Hegelian double negation (not only to negate the unjust concrete problems of individuals or groups, but also the structures that produced them) and a Marxist political economy points towards a society where the dark sides of capitalism do not reign. The problem that we are confronted with, is that it is currently very difficult to make this society present even as an option. Nonetheless, it must be attempted. When Žižek, after a public lecture in the US, was forced by an angry person in the audience to answer the question about what kind of society it is that he wants, but never talks about, he answered with a seemingly surprised exclamation: 'Communism, of course!' In fact, this approach to Marxism is not that different from Marx and Engels themselves. In *German Ideology*, it is thus written:

> Communism is for us not a *state of affairs* which is to be established, an *ideal* to which reality [will] have to adjust itself. We call communism the *real* movement which abolishes the present state of things. The conditions of this movement result from the premises now in existence. (Marx 1975)

In any case, Žižek is an important voice in the reintroduction of Marxism that has gained some momentum in recent years – not least since the global financial crisis broke out in 2008. His questioning of capitalism has a number of acute points that are difficult to dismiss, and he seems to be part of a broader theoretical endeavour to prepare a new program for the left, rather than to merely repeat old, leftist dogma. And it still very much makes sense to distinguish between left and right, although it is sometimes denied. Let us, in order to summarise some of the main points of this and the preceding chapter, quote Žižek's elaboration of this distinction.

> While the Right legitimizes its suspension of the Ethical by its anti-universalist stance – that is, by a reference to its particular (religious patriotic) identity which overrules any universal moral or legal standards – the Left legitimizes its suspension of the Ethical precisely by means of a reference to the true Universality to come. Or – to put it another way – the Left simultaneously accepts the antagonistic character of society (there is no neutral position, struggle is constitutive) *and* remains universalist (speaking on behalf of universal emancipation): in the leftish perspective, accepting the radically antagonistic – that is, *political* – character of social life, accepting the necessity of 'taking sides', is the only way to be effectively *universal*. (Žižek 1999: 223f)

Žižek claims that there are two dominant ways of relating to the Marxist heritage within the left. He illustrates these through two English films from the 1990s: *Brassed Off* and *The Full Monty*. Both of these films tell the story of the disintegration of classical working class identity. In *Brassed Off*, a group of miners protest against the plans to close their mine due to it no longer being economically feasible. The miners' struggle finds an expression through their brass band. Even though the mine does in fact close down, the miners keep playing the old tunes of the working class, knowing very well that their struggle has been lost. In the other film, *The Full Monty*, a group of unemployed workers are depicted who are trying to create a new life for themselves by learning how to strip. They are not, like in *Brassed Off*, trying to hold on to the old values and routines, but rather disclaiming any reference to the macho identity of the working class, or to the working class as such. Is not the contemporary left plagued by a similar dilemma?

> So, in today's leftist politics, we seem in effect to be reduced to the choice between the 'solid' orthodox attitude of proudly,

out of principle, sticking to the old (Communist or Social
Democratic) tune, although we know its time has passed, and
the New Labour 'radical centre' attitude of going the 'full
Monty' in stripping, getting rid of, the last vestiges of proper
leftist discourse. (Žižek 1999: 353)

Žižek points to a third way beyond the orthodoxy and the denial of the Marxist tradition respectively, a way which involves a rereading of the tradition as a tradition for radical critique. Even though capitalism seems to be all inclusive and inevitable, we may still hope for a miracle. Žižek's message is that this miracle begins from the subject. The miracle, revolution, takes as its point of departure the revolutionary, dare we say Cartesian, subject. The imperative is to give Descartes' famous *dictum* an activist turn: *I struggle, therefore I can become more than I am.*

Chapter 5. Did somebody say totalitarianism? Žižek's critics.

Slavoj Žižek's first major work in English, *The Sublime Object of Ideology* from 1989, was introduced by Ernesto Laclau. In his preface, Laclau identified the 'Slovenian Lacanian School' as one that was outlining 'the main characteristics of radical democratic struggles in Eastern European societies' (Laclau 1989: xi), and emphasised the philosophical and political convergence between his own and Žižek's positions in the common struggle for 'constructing a democratic socialist political project in a post-Marxist age' (ibid.: xv). Žižek, in the book, indeed emphasises that democracy means the inexistence of the People on behalf of which some representative could legitimately rule. No one is entitled to claim the right to occupy political power on the basis of an ultimate and flawless vision of the perfect society. In liberal democracies, elections therefore function as 'an act of dissolution' of the social edifice: 'the whole hierarchic network of social relations is in a way suspended, put in parentheses; 'society' as an organic unity ceases to exist, it changes into a contingent collection of atomized individuals' (Žižek 1989: 148).

If the Lacanian Real is that which resists symbolisation, one could say that in political terms, the Real marks the 'impossibility of any ultimate suture of society', as Laclau would have put it (Daly 1999: 220). An 'ultimate suture' meaning here a way of 'healing' or closing society such that everything is explained, taken care of, and cannot be undone. Power, in liberal democracy, must, because of the impossibility of an ultimate suture, be calibrated by the potential opening for that which is not represented at any given time. We have never reached the 'final stage' where those in power can remain in power on the basis of their access to truth, and free elections mark this impossibility of the perfect political symbolisation. By thus 'institutionalising' the Real, so to speak, as the empty seats of parliament, liberal democracy always keeps the place of power open for new democratic struggles. Initially, Laclau and Žižek shared the emphasis on this fundamental necessity of liberal democracy.

The rebellion against the father

In 2003, Žižek was portrayed by Astra Taylor in a biographical documentary (appropriately entitled *Žižek!*), where he denounced the earlier 'radical democratic' view. 'I am more and more self-critical of the first one', he commented, (referring to *The Sublime Object of Ideology*), and added that the problem lies exactly in the emphasis on democracy, pluralism and critique of totalitarian ideology. Žižek has not become anti-democratic since 1989, and certainly not a defender of any of the totalitarian regimes of the twentieth century, but he has turned his political attention away from the emphasis on the dangers of a closed or 'sutured' explicit ideology and turned partly towards a critique of the types of ideological structures that function precisely on the basis of people being well aware that there is no such thing as a harmonic, sutured unity of society, and partly towards an investigation of types of political action or events that are not first and foremost democratic, but are first and foremost required.

Glyn Daly, who is one of Žižek's more recent allies, has described the difference between two conceptions of ideology in a way that fits nicely to the change Žižek has undergone in his turn away from Ernesto Laclau and Chantal Mouffe's critique of ideology. '[T]he central problem is not so much,' as Daly writes, 'that society is *logically* impossible [...] but that, at the level of *fantasy*, society is regarded *as possible*; as something which is ultimately achievable through a certain overcoming of specified impedances' (Daly 1999: 224). This understanding of ideology has already been scrutinised, but we bring it up here again to emphasise the difference that is now more apparent to the 'radical democratic' view of ideology in Laclau and Mouffe. Žižek is not so much interested in demonstrating how ideologies are explicit, hegemonic discourses that offer subjects a unified picture of society as he is in how ideology is sustained, *even though* its subjects are 'enlightened', critical subjects that know very well…

A natural consequence of this change of perspective is that political normativity also changes focus. If Žižek, in the early work, devotes more energy to analysing and criticising any party or movement that considers itself to offer an 'ultimate suture' of society, he is now much more interested in types of political action that allow us to escape from the fantasmatic belief in society that structures our very social reality – democratic, enlightened, critical, or not. The problem is that the 'radical democratic' project of pluralism, liberalism, and open ended political structures without totalitarian sutures seems to function very well with cynical or unconscious attachments to fantasmatically structured enjoyment that nonetheless sustains relations of exploitation, devastation of the natural environment, bio-political measures towards a society of surveillance, and so on. We know very well that society is logically impossible, but we nonetheless continue to behave as if it were possible, because at the level of fantasy we still secretly believe it is. To end exploitation and suppression, therefore, it does not suffice to advocate liberal, open-ended structures and enlighten people about the impossibility of ultimate sutures.

Another, more radical, type of action is needed (one that is literally more radical than radical democracy), and since the thing that keeps us hanging on to the status quo of the current (political) state of affairs is enjoyment sustained on the unconscious level, Žižek quite logically seeks models of action in psychoanalysis. In psychoanalysis we find various descriptions of that which allows us to break free from pathological bindings – something which requires an act on behalf of the analysand, a way of passing from the passive, analysed subject, to the active, liberated subject. This passage, however, is one that cannot be warranted from within the structures that are being interpreted – it is exactly supposed to finish off the particular chain of signification within which everything formerly made sense. Therefore, the act that Žižek is after has a clear ring of rupture, violence and lack of legitimacy (within the confines of the prevailing morality, culture, political framework). It is in an important sense impossible – it cannot happen, but it happens nonetheless. Ian Parker, who has written a critical introduction to Žižek, sees in this quest for the liberating act a serious exaggeration of the psychoanalytic notions of act, and emphasises how there is...

> ... an opposition structuring Žižek's writing, an opposition between the option of moving in or moving out. This opposition sets out a forced choice: an embrace of the way things are as the conservative option, or escape from everything, as the ultra-left option. (Parker 2004: 124)

Žižek now, to some, appears as someone who has become almost obsessed with rupture, transgression and revolution – as if everything but the radical overturning of the prevailing political order were mere complacency, pseudo-activity and ultimately cynical maintenance of the status quo (at the expense of someone else). Laclau himself has mockingly described this 'new' radical Žižek as someone so occupied by monumental acts that he can hardly even say the word 'r-r-revolution' without stuttering and chanting. Žižek wants to 'do away with liberal democratic regimes,' Laclau says, but unfortunately, he does not 'have the courtesy of letting us know anything about' what he plans to have them replaced by (Laclau 2000: 289).

For Laclau, furthermore, Žižek seems to have regressed, rather than developed, to a stage of Marxist thinking that most scholars have otherwise considered outdated since the collapse of the socialist regimes.

Laclau and Mouffe's influential 1985 work *Hegemony and Socialist Strategy* was in many ways exactly a departure from traditional Marxist thinking and particularly, in the eyes of the authors, from the understanding of class struggle in purely economic terms and as the determining factor of social struggle and historical development: in *the last instance*, as it was typically called. Žižek's return to Marxism precisely implies a return to thinking capital as the fundamental engine and determining factor in society, as the Real underlying any superstructure narratives of multiculturalism, postmodernism, identity politics, etc. But Žižek never offers an actual economic analysis of the ways in which capital works, and therefore his repeated emphasis that 'it's the economy, stupid', tends to be viewed as a cheap trick in the eyes of many commentators – not least in

Ernesto Laclau's.

Combined with the emphasis on act and revolution, Žižek's political analysis of contemporary capitalist society contains a rather noticeable amount of gestures and imperatives that are hard to follow in real life. While Žižek himself seems to believe that this is a necessary postponement because we have not yet reached an historical point that allows us to clearly identify new paths for political action, his opponents are much more prone to seeing his double lack (lack of economic analysis and lack of political alternative) as a sign of either analytical immaturity or a (not-so-innocent) romantic longing for the good old days of violent uprising and mayhem.

Passions of the real

So, let us take a short look at Žižek's view on violence. In his 2008 book on violence, Žižek distinguishes between three main categories of violence: subjective, objective (subdivided in symbolic and systemic) and divine. The two former forms are distinguished by the presence or absence of a clearly identifiable agent behind the act. Subjective violence is the type of violence that is performed by an agent (a subject) with or without malicious intent, but with a clear, causal responsibility for harm or danger bestowed on others. If I punch you in the face it was clearly me that was the subject behind the pain inflicted and I can be held responsible and probably punished according to prevailing law. Objective violence, on the other hand, is impossible to attribute to any one separate agent. It is the type of violence that is 'inherent' in the ways things are functioning, and as such there is no 'outside' from where it can be judged and penalised.

Objective violence is the unforeseen or unintended effects of systems that are functioning well in other respects. Global capitalism is the clearest example here – the unfortunate sufferings and poverty in Third World countries are often seen as something comparable to collateral damage, while the relative affluence and comfort of citizens in rich countries are seen as justified and reasonable, and never the twain shall be causally linked. How can I, working honestly and consuming peacefully like the next man, be held responsible for tragedies occurring far away? In terms of subjective violence, I cannot. There is (mostly) no direct link between someone buying a relatively innocent stock in some relatively innocent company, and people suffering from economic and social tragedies in places that might be 'connected' to the world market in ways that are only indirectly relevant to the stock holder in the North. Nonetheless, something does violate the opportunities and rights of a great number of poor people around the world. This 'something' is the agent behind objective violence – which cannot be symbolised (which is why Žižek calls capitalism the Real of the contemporary age of globalisation). Objective violence is the type of violence that 'just happens' and is rarely spoken of *as* violence.

Therefore, the first task identified by Žižek in *Violence* is that we must learn to 'take a step back' and see the overall picture in order to understand the types of violence that are inflicted without anyone being individually responsible for them. In the current discussions of climate change, isn't this exactly the task that is still to be resolved? We must step back and clarify how suffering is inflicted across the world by an immensely complex network of effects from human activities that have been seen as perfectly innocent until fairly recently. Anonymously benefiting from tragedies only indirectly inferred by us, we thus all participate in objective violence without being held responsible for it.

The second task, then, is to improve our understanding of events that are generally treated as 'subjective' violence, but according to Žižek might be more correctly understood as 'divine'. He borrows the latter term from German philosopher Walter Benjamin (1892–1940), who in his 'Critique of Violence' used this concept to describe a type of justified violence that tears down all barriers and limits and is 'law-destroying' (Benjamin 1996: 249). Benjamin develops his concept of divine violence in opposition to what he calls 'mythic' violence, which is the law-establishing violence that establishes limits and barriers and makes it possible for anything to be considered (by humans) to be right or wrong.

Paraphrasing Benjamin, you could say that it is because of some mythic deeds in the past that we have society and the possibility of identifying something as (what Žižek calls) subjective violence at all. Because of mythic violence, we have a legal order within which something is right and something wrong. More concretely, the founding of any legal order necessarily entails acts of violence. Minimally (take the case of a peaceful political revolution), founding an order is an act of *symbolic* violence: that which is now considered right was formerly not right at all. To have a legal order, you must *make* something legal (and illegal). Law is therefore, in its essence, universalised crime, as Žižek says. But the foundation of a legal order might of course also include acts of *physical* violence, like beheading the king, to establish a new monopoly of violence. In any case, Benjamin seems, by mythic violence, to refer to the inscrutable origins of the current state, or to the natural inclination in the inhabitants of the current state to consider the origins of the prevailing order as naturally justified and based on heroic deeds of the past. They are mythic, because they cannot be justified from inside the legal order in question but are the very condition of anything being justifiable.

When Benjamin nonetheless talks of divine violence, he opens the field for what one must conceive as a 'higher justice', i.e. the abolishment of the framework of what counts as justified on behalf of something that is more or above the current order. Because it comes from 'above', divine violence does not comply with the standards and regulations of what is right and wrong within the legal order. It represents a type of justice that cannot be reduced to the contingent standards currently in place, and divine violence is therefore without standards or measurements or concepts of more or less. It simply annihilates the current standards – rebels against them in the name of a pure, unspeakable universal justice. Žižek paraphrases Benjamin thus: '"Divine violence" stands for such brutal intrusions of justice beyond law' (Žižek 2008: 151), and he challenges his readers to consider possible actual examples of such intrusions that should be counted as divine (ibid.: 167).

The one example that he himself devotes the most attention is the case of the riots in Paris in 2005. According to Žižek, the sudden outburst of violence in the streets of Paris could be described in terms of Benjamin's concept, because they were in a specific sense beyond signification. A big group of mainly younger Muslim immigrants stirred up the public scene by setting cars on fire, putting up barricades, etc., but not with a clear statement of what they demanded in return for stopping the violence or even what they were 'protesting' against. 'The riots were simply a direct effort to gain visibility. [...] Their actions spoke for them: like it or not, we're here, no matter how much you pretend not to see us.' (ibid.: 65).

There are different ways of criticising Žižek for some of the interpretations in *Violence*. One of them, as is sometimes the case with this particular author, would be to conduct a simple empirical investigation of what took place. The apparent speechlessness of the actors in Paris was, for instance, put in question by a group of editors who published a book, relatively shortly after, with the telling title *Une révolte en toute logique*, i.e. 'an entirely logical revolt' (Berger et. al. 2006). The book contains, among other contributions and documents, a series of interviews with some of the people who participated in the tumultuous events of 2005, thereby displaying a keen sense of a series of background issues that were behind the eruptions of violence that might have seemed like meaningless destruction to most people from the outside.

Secondly, Žižek seems to be contradicting himself already in his own analysis. On the one hand, the riots were totally devoid of any positive message (in agreement with Benjamin's concept); on the other they were expressions of a quite specific message – 'we are here' – which is already an expression that necessarily relies on a series of implicit preconditions: a lack of rights to certain groups in French society, particularly the so called *sens papiers* (those 'without documents'), a lack of awareness of this situation among the general public and/or a reluctance against accepting information about the 'real state of affairs' among the young immigrants. In other words: regardless of whether the riots were in fact *une révolte en toute logique*, Žižek does explicitly and implicitly attribute meaning to them in ways that cannot but be said to contradict Benjamin's original concept of divine violence.

One could argue that this does not necessarily constitute an insurmountable problem for Žižek, considering the fact that he does not have problems with 'short circuiting' classical texts, and looking for what you could maybe term a secular, psychoanalytically informed conception of 'divine violence' with appropriate deconstructive quotation marks. One possible route for such an endeavour could be to make sense of a modified concept of 'divine violence' that would mean something like 'apparently meaningless violent actions that must be interpreted and put into context in order to extract the meaning that they will-have-had.' This means: maybe we are not able to express at the moment of the act, whether 'from inside' or 'from outside' what is 'right' about some outbursts of rage and contempt, but they nonetheless contain something – a message from the future, if you will, about what is wrong with the current state of affairs. If an act is an act of 'divine violence', in other words, then the message it contains will become clear at a subsequent stage without the agent being consciously aware of it. In this way, one could even talk of a new type of hermeneutics of violence that could be put to use to interpret events and riots that otherwise seem to escape understanding.

Žižek's more principled critics, however, seem to have been on the lookout for some years for proof of his radical, anti-democratic, and potentially r-r-r-revolutionary stance, and some of them seem to have found this proof in *Violence*. One quite harsh exchange on the subject of violence followed between Žižek and British critic Simon Critchley after the latter reviewed *Violence* in *The Independent* (Critchley 2008). Critchley identified the same seeming paradox (like Ian Parker and Ernesto Laclau) in Žižek between the urge for radical action and the complete absence of concrete ideas or initiatives. This paradox in Žižek particularly tends to provoke people like Critchley who try to think more concretely about commitment, resistance and action, because Žižek rarely steps back from an opportunity to ridicule their efforts as pseudo-activism or as 'surrender' to the workings of the liberal capitalist hegemony. Philosophers have long wanted to change the world, as Žižek likes to invert Marx' famous motto, what is needed is to interpret it. Sometimes the best thing to do is to do nothing, or, at the most, to sit down and write philosophy in order to come closer to an understanding of the objective measures of the world.

The endless amounts of interpretations from Žižek's hand, however, have not yet produced anything like an answer to the old question 'what should be done?', and it sometimes seems that the closest we will ever come to an answer will be an injunction to wait and prepare ourselves. Žižek's politics, on an ungenerous interpretation, could be said to consist in the old wisdom in Western movies about not shooting before you see the white in their eyes, although in Žižek's case, the enemy seems never to come close enough. 'The moment' will come, but it is (always) not quite here yet, and until then it is best to sit still.

Critchley is more blunt: 'the truth is that Žižek is never ready', and he ends up 'diagnosing' Žižek, in an unusually personal manner, as an obsessive neurotic, manically producing books, articles and lectures, while secretly dreaming of divine violence, 'a cataclysmic, purifying violence of the sovereign ethical deed', one for which, however, 'he lacks the courage' (ibid.). Critchley's personal and rather emotional attack does display some of the inherent tensions in Žižek's work, although it is so exaggerated that it hardly adds to the understanding of the oeuvre. The two have clear and unquestionable differences both politically and philosophically, which obviously places them in opposing camps. But it seems to be quite an extraordinary move to turn such disagreements on political and philosophical theory into a vindictive search for pathological motives in the opponent. It seems like Critchley is systematically and deliberately failing to understand Žižek's gesture in some of his 'radical' statements.

As Jodi Dean has shown (Dean 2006), Žižek's strategy in political discussions is to take the position of the analyst (rather than that of the master) and try to confront/provoke his readers and audience with issues in our own strategies for not taking action, not imagining radically different politically scenarios than the current ones, not seriously taking the economical injustices of the world into consideration, and so on. This is done, it should of course be noted, on a social or cultural level, rather than on a personal level (like that of Critchley's 'analysis' of Žižek). Žižek reads signs in public discourse, political decisions, writings, popular culture, etc. as indications of the 'state of mind' of contemporary society, and not least of the unspoken messages that circulate beneath the surface of the official rhetoric. Whenever he identifies an issue of denial or repression in public or philosophical discourse, he generally attacks with reinforced imperatives of real political change rather than half hearted encouragement to, for instance, ameliorate the harsh conditions in poor countries.

His strategy is often to show that the conditions we are trying to improve or prevent are created by the very same economical system from which we benefit on a daily level, which means that the real signification of acts of benevolence, philanthropy and care, is sometimes almost the exact opposite of what was (consciously) intended: being able to continue enjoying, while maintaining a picture of ourselves as good, honest and engaged people. Take fair trade, for example: isn't it possible that we are purchasing fair trade products much more because we want to 'send a signal' to friends, colleagues, etc., about our own ethical values, than because we actually have in mind the living conditions of some Central American farmer? Or even: does it change his living conditions, even if we do in fact 'have him in mind'? Whenever Žižek identifies types of action that make the agents 'feel good about themselves' without seriously challenging political and economical power, he immediately becomes sceptical about its real political value and tends to dismiss it as pseudo-activism.

The demonstrations against the war in Iraq make another nice example of this type of critique: while demonstrators across the Western world vehemently protested against the already settled decision of the 'coalition of the willing' to engage in a war against Saddam Hussein's regime, the planning and execution of the war could proceed almost entirely undisturbed. The tacit deal between the two parties was: we are allowed to distance ourselves from the tragic outcomes of the war, while you are allowed to continue planning it. American president George W. Bush, the *de facto* leader of the coalition, made a similar point when he proclaimed that the demonstrations were an excellent example of the individual liberties that everyone enjoys in the free world and that this was exactly what he was hoping to introduce in Iraq as well.

The useful idiot

At the heart of the exchange with Simon Critchley, nonetheless, lies the question of whether the left should 'bombard' the state with impossible demands and always work on the margins of official policy or whether it should work for a take over of state power. Žižek remains sceptical of any indication of resignation on the left. In his opinion, stepping back from class struggle in the sense of a very real struggle for political power that doesn't necessarily respect the rules of the current political game (liberal capitalist democracy) is roughly identical to giving up on political struggle as such. And Žižek's diagnosis of his time is that this is largely the state of mind we are all in. On numerous occasions, he has illustrated this by a simple comparison: it is relatively easy for most of us to imagine some natural disaster or cosmic event (meteors, asteroids, comets) that would exterminate all life on the planet. But imagining a serious change of the political coordinates in which we live is almost entirely impossible; a small, radical change in the economic conditions and regulations around the globe. It is not only Žižek who 'has no alternative', it is not even only the Left that hasn't – it is basically all of us who are paralysed by the headlights of global capitalism.

Žižek's opposition, therefore, is opposition on the level of thinking: we at least cannot allow ourselves to give up the ability to examine, scrutinise and seek new ways of seeing ourselves and our societies; this would mean resignation in a much more tragic sense than it might immediately appear. If the frame is set, once and for all, political change remains 'political change without political change', and giving up the perspective of political change is not only a way of maintaining the 'objective violence' of the way things are running, but also a way of refraining from *thinking* (politically). The title of his reply to Critchley's book *Infinitely Demanding* (2007) encapsulates this scepticism rather precisely: 'Resistance is Surrender'. If you are 'obsessed' (to use Critchley's own wording against himself) with demonstrating your dissatisfaction with the current state of affairs, you might very well be secretly wishing for them to basically remain as they are. In this precise sense, it is better not to do anything, to stay at home and read philosophy, than to display resistance against the state in the streets with banners and slogans.

The emphasis on 'real' political action therefore forces Žižek to risk identifying deeds that are disputed and controversial as possible eye-opening examples of what is required to really change something. His investigations of some of the laudable aspects of historical figures like Robespierre, Lenin, Stalin, Mao and Hugo Chavez are examples of this insistence on the revolutionary act that was discussed in chapter 4. In Astra Taylor's documentary, Žižek is portrayed in the entrance of his apartment in Ljubljana in front of a poster with Stalin that says 'Welcome to Socialist Welfare'. Here, he reluctantly admits that he is 'of course not a Stalinist', which would be stupid and vulgar, but that he nonetheless insists on bringing such excessive figures into debates, because 'the message would not get through', if he merely repeated the same moderate song that everyone is singing about respect, tolerance, democracy, equality, etc. In order to bring forward the real political issues, one must be ready to take on a certain excessive posture and seek an opening into something that was not considered possible.

And the same goes for actual political practice. History does give examples of events and acts that really change the political landscape and make possible what had not even been thought before. The revolutions of France and Russia, the civil rights movement, even President Obama's election in the USA (although on another scale) represent occasions where something that could not happen nonetheless took place. In the case of Russia, Žižek's point is that although the socialism of the twentieth century failed miserably (a point which he repeated in BBC's Hardtalk on 24 November, 2009), the revolution nonetheless opened a field of politics that made it possible to see the standards according to which it unfortunately and tragically failed.

When analysing acts that have some of the revolutionary potential or momentum that Žižek believes is required, he does embody some of the traits of what, for instance, conservative US columnist Mona Charen has called 'the useful idiots' who are always 'blaming America first' and condoning the revolutionary acts of despots around the world (Charen 2004). The term 'useful idiots' is usually (although probably falsely) attributed to Vladimir Lenin who allegedly used it to describe the journalists and intellectuals in the West who were speaking about the cause of the Bolsheviks without being aware of the real agenda that would be enforced once they seized power. The description fits Žižek because he is in fact always more concerned with the black holes in our own self-understanding than he is with condemning or critically analysing regimes and figures that are generally considered to be a threat to 'our way of life'.

To use the proverbial uncanny scene from horror movies, 'the call is coming from within the house' that Žižek's analyzes; he is the voice that immediately and logically must come from the outside, because it appears as a foreign voice or even a threat, although he is every bit as much 'inside the house' as the people he is criticising. We pick up the phone and hear a radical rhetoric in a strangely distorted accent, only to find out that the voice is coming from right next to us. Žižek is trying to bring out the unacknowledged beliefs that structure our social reality and political systems and, in so doing, he often makes examples from despots and 'evil' regimes seem like logical replies to the structures of domination and repression that 'we' have bestowed on them, if not simply taking their acts as exemplary of genuine political conviction. It is not so surprising, perhaps, that this accusing voice sometimes seems to be excessive or dangerous or even a 'useful' instrument of our enemy's intentions of bringing down everything we hold dear. But one could also turn the table and ask if it is not exactly such useful idiots who are always remarkably absent in regimes of the sort that 'we' are generally afraid of and not so seldom actively combating – Stalin's USSR, Saddam Hussein's Iraq, Kim Jong-il's North Korea, or Afghanistan under Taleban rule. One should therefore add to the designation of someone as a useful idiot: 'useful – to whom?' and be ready for a surprising answer.

Bibliography

Althusser, Louis (1984): *Essays on Ideology*, London: Verso.

Benjamin, Walter (1996): 'Critique of Violence', Cambridge, Massachussetts: Harvard University Press.

Berger et.al. (eds.) (2006): *Une rèvolte en toute logique*, Paris: L'Archipel des Pirates.

Charen, Mona (2004): *Useful Idiots – How Liberals Got It Wrong in the Cold War and Still Blame America First*, Washington: HarperCollins Publishers.

Critchley, Simon (2007): *Infinitely Demanding. Ethics of Commitment. Politics of Resistance*, London: Verso.

Critchley, Simon (2008): 'Violence, By Slavoj Žižek', *The Independent* (11 January).

Daly, Glyn (1999): 'Ideology and its Paradoxes: Dimensions of Fantasy and Enjoyment', Journal of Political Ideologies, 4 (2): 219–238.

Daly, Glyn & Slavoj Žižek (2004): *Conversations with Žižek*, Cambridge: Polity Press.

Dean, Jodi (2006): *Žižek's Politics*, New York: Routledge.

Dolar, Mladen (1993): 'Beyond Interpellation', *Qui Parle*, 6 (2): 75–96.

Dolar, Mladen (1998). 'Cogito as the Subject of the Unconscious', in Renata Salecl and Slavoj Žižek (red.): *Cogito and the Unconscious, SIC 2*. Durham: Duke University Press, p. 11–40.

Freud, Sigmund (1999 [1942]): *Die Traumdeutung*, Gesammelte Werke II/III, Frankfurt am Main: Fischer Taschenbuch Verlag.

Fukuyama, Francis (1992): *The End of History and the Last Man*. London: Penguin.

Heidegger, Martin (1993 [1927]): *Sein und Zeit*. Tübingen: Max Niemeyer Verlag.

Helmer, Oscar & Slavoj Žižek (1995): 'Venstresiden bør lære av fundamentalisterne!', *Samtiden*, 6: 14–23.

Hughes, Robert (1999 [1993]): *The Culture of Complaint*. London: The Harvill Press.

Hyldgaard, Kirsten (1998). *Fantasien til afmagten. Syv kapitler om Lacan og filosofien*. København: Museum Tusculanums Forlag.

Kymlicka, Will (1995): *Multicultural Citizenship*. Oxford: Clarendon Press

Lacan, Jacques (1977 [1966]): 'The mirror stage as formative of the function of the I'. In *Écrits*, London: Routledge, pp. 1–7.

Marx, Karl (1975 [1845–6]): *German Ideology*, London: Lawrence & Wishart.

Marx, Karl & Frederich Engels (1998 [1848]): *The Communist Manifesto*. London: Verso.

Mead, Rebecca: 'The Marx Brother'. *The New Yorker* (5.5.2003).

Mortensen, Nils (2003): *Det paradoksale samfund*. København: Hans Reitzels Forlag.

Parker, Ian (2004): *Slavoj Žižek – A Critical Introduction*, London: Pluto Press.

Riha, Rado (1993): *Reale Geschehnisse der Freiheit*. Wien: Turia + Kant.

Rösing, Lilian Munk (2005): 'Psykoanalyse – Lacans formalisering af Freud', in Niels Åkerstrøm Andersen, Anders Esmark & Carsten Bagge Laustsen (red.), *Poststrukturalistiske analysestrategier*. København: Roskilde Universitetsforlag, pp. 97–125.

Young, Iris (1989): 'Polity and Group Difference: A Critique of the Ideal of Universal Citizenship', *Ethics*, 99 (2): 250–274.

Žižek, Slavoj (1989): *The Sublime Object of Ideology*. London: Verso.

Žižek, Slavoj (1991a): *For they know not what they do – Enjoyment as a political factor*. London: Verso.

Žižek, Slavoj (1991b): *Looking Awry – An Introduction to Jacques Lacan through Popular Culture.* Massachusetts: The MIT Press.

Žižek, Slavoj (1992a): *Enjoy Your Symptom! Jacques Lacan in Hollywood and out.* London: Routledge.

Žižek, Slavoj (1992b): 'In His Bold Gaze My Ruin Writ Large'. In Slavoj Žižek (red.): *Everything You Always Wanted to Know about Lacan (But Were Afraid to Ask Hitchcock).* London: Verso, pp. 211–272.

Žižek, Slavoj (1993a): *Tarrying with the Negative – Kant, Hegel, and the Critique of Ideology.* Durham: Duke University Press.

Žižek, Slavoj (1993b): 'Caught in Another's Dream in Bosnia'. In Rabia Ali & Lawrence Lifschultz (red.): *Why Bosnia?* Stony Creek, Ct.: Pamphleteer's Press, pp. 233–240.

Žižek, Slavoj (1994a): 'The Spectre of Ideology'. In Slavoj Žižek (red.), *Mapping Ideology.* London: Verso, pp. 1–33.

Žižek, Slavoj (1994b): *The Metastases of Enjoyment – Six Essays on Woman and Causality.* London: Verso.

Žižek, Slavoj (1996): *The Indivisible Remainder – Essays on Schelling and Related Matters.* London: Verso.

Žižek, Slavoj (1997): *The Plague of Fantasies.* London: Verso.

Žižek, Slavoj (1999): *The Ticklish Subject. The absent centre of political ontology*, London: Verso.

Žižek, Slavoj (2000a): 'Class Struggle or Postmodernism? Yes Please!'. In Judith Butler, Ernesto Laclau and Slavoj Žižek: *Contingency, Hegemony, Universality. Contemporary Dialogues on the Left.* London: Verso, pp. 90–135.

Žižek, Slavoj (2000b): *The Fragile Absolute – or, why is the Christian legacy worth fighting for?* London: Verso.

Žižek, Slavoj (2000c): 'Holding the Place'. In Judith Butler, Ernesto Laclau and Slavoj Žižek: *Contingency, Hegemony, Universality: Contemporary Dialogues on the Left.* London: Verso, pp. 308–329.

Žižek, Slavoj (2001a): *Did Somebody Say Totalitarianism? Five Interventions in the (Mis)use of a Notion.* London: Verso.

Žižek, Slavoj (2001b): '*Welcome to the Desert of the Real*', http://web.mit.edu/cms/reconstructions/interpretations/desertreal.html

Žižek, Slavoj (2001c): *On Belief*. London: Routledge.

Žižek, Slavoj (2001d): 'The Rhetorics of Power', *Diacritics*, 31 (1): 91–104.

Žižek, Slavoj (2002a): *Welcome to the Desert of the Real*. London: Verso.

Žižek, Slavoj (2002b): *Revolution at the Gates. Selected Writings of Lenin From 1917*. London: Verso.

Žižek, Slavoj (2003): *The Puppet and the Dwarf. The Perverse Core of Christianity*. Cambridge: The MIT Press.

Žižek, Slavoj (2004): *Iraq. The borrowed kettle*. London: Verso.

Žižek, Slavoj (2006): 'Defenders of the Faith', *New York Times*, 3.12.

Žižek, Slavoj (2008): *Violence*, London: Profile Books.

Zupančič, Alenka (2000): *Ethics of the Real: Kant, Lacan*. London: Verso.

Humanities Insights

These are some of the Insights available at:
http://www.humanities-ebooks.co.uk/
and MyiLibrary.com and (in most cases) from Kindle

General Titles

Modern Feminist Theory
An Introduction to Critical Theory
An Introduction to Rhetorical Terms

Genre Fiction Sightlines

Octavia E Butler: *Xenogenesis / Lilith's Brood*
Reginal Hill: *On Beulah's Height*
Ian McDonald: *Chaga / Evolution's Store*
Walter Mosley: *Devil in a Blue Dress*
Tamora Pierce: *The Immortals*

History Insights

Oliver Cromwell
The British Empire: Pomp, Power and Postcolonialism
The Holocaust: Events, Motives, Legacy *
Lenin's Revolution
Methodism and Society
The Risorgimento

Philosophy Insights

American Pragmatism
Barthes
Critical Thinking & Informal Logic
Existentialism
Formal Logic
MetaEthics *
Contemporary Philosophy of Religion *
Philosophy of Sport
Plato
Wittgenstein

* also in paperback from Troubador.co.uk

www.ingramcontent.com/pod-product-compliance
Ingram Content Group UK Ltd.
Pitfield, Milton Keynes, MK11 3LW, UK
UKHW041435180426
11947UKWH00007B/466